The Practice of
Spiritual Direction

The Practice of Spiritual Direction

William A. Barry
and William J. Connolly

THE SEABURY PRESS

TO OUR PARENTS
William Barry and Catherine McKenna Barry
Eugene A. Connolly and Catherine Menut Connolly
Whose faith and hope and love made the
Mystery a tangible reality in our lives

Library of Congress Card Catalog Number: 81-14566
ISBN: 0-86683- 951-8 (previously ISBN: 0-8164-2357-1)

Printed in the United States of America
5   4   3   2   1

The Seabury Press
430 Oak Grove
Minneapolis, Minnesota 55403

We gratefully acknowledge permission to adapt and reprint the following material. Parts of Chapters 1, 3, 4, 7, 8, and 9 originally appeared in William J. Connolly, "Contemporary Spiritual Direction: Scope and Principles. An Introductory Essay," *Studies in the Spirituality of Jesuits* 7, no. 3 (1975), published by the American Assistancy Seminar on Jesuit Spirituality, St. Louis, Mo., and William J. Connolly, "Appealing to Strength in Spiritual Direction," *Review for Religious* 32(1973): 1060–1063

Part of Chapter 5 originally appeared in William J. Connolly, "Noticing Key Interior Facts in the Early Stages of Spiritual Direction," *Review for Religious* 35 (1976): 112–121.

Part of Chapter 4 originally appeared in William A. Barry, "The Contemplative Attitude in Spiritual Direction," *Review for Religious* 35 (1976): 820–828. Also reprinted in David L. Fleming, ed., *Notes on the Spiritual Exercises of St. Ignatius of Loyola* (St. Louis: Review for Religious, 1981), pp. 52–60.

Part of Chapter 8 originally appeared in William A. Barry, "The Prior Experience of Spiritual Directors," *Spiritual Life* 22 (1977): 84–89.

Part of Chapter 11 originally appeared in William A. Barry and Mary C. Guy, "The Practice of Supervision in Spiritual Direction," *Review for Religious* 37 (1978): 834–842.

Quotations from Scripture are from the Revised Standard Version of the Bible. Copyright © 1946, 1952, Division of Christian Education of the National Council of the Churches of Christ in the U.S.A.

Contents

Preface

During the last ten years spiritual direction has gained a surprising currency in Christian circles. Many more people, both Protestant and Roman Catholic, know about it. Many more are engaged in it, both as directors and directees, than was the case in previous decades. Moreover, where once the great majority of those who sought spiritual direction were Roman Catholic members of religious orders and seminarians, and the great majority of those who gave spiritual direction were Roman Catholic priests, today there is diversity: Protestants and Roman Catholics, lay men and women, priests, ministers, religious sisters and brothers. The kind of person who seeks direction also seems to have changed. Fewer people who live routine lives and more people who live varied, active, and unconventional lives now come for direction.

Not only are more people, and people of more varied backgrounds, looking for and giving direction. In the past five years there has been a remarkable increase in the discussion of spirituality and spiritual direction. Workshops and courses on prayer and direction for priests, ministers, sisters, brothers, and seminarians have become more available. Training programs for spiritual directors and service centers for spiritual direction have been established in a number of places. A steadily increasing number of articles and books on prayer, spirituality, and the art of spiritual direction have been published. This is a very different situation from that of the late sixties and earlier when such workshops, training programs, and books were virtually or completely unknown.

This book, then, has been written in the midst of a period of enthusiasm for spirituality and spiritual direction. One of the best results of such periods is their promotion of new interest in fields that were little known up to that time and the increased information they have made available about those fields. If the present interest in spiritual direction follows the course of other recent movements in American spirituality, the enthusiasm itself will not last more than ten years or so. During that time, however, study and research of permanent value for both spiritual theology and spiritual direction can be accomplished. The temporary phenomenon of enthusiasm can bring about solid evaluation of the benefits of direction and a knowledgeable discrimination among approaches to it.

We would like this book to be a contribution to such a critical evaluation. We do not propose that spiritual direction is a necessary means for growing in spiritual life. Nor do we propose that it is always helpful. We suggest only that direction be judged by people's experience of it and not simply on a priori grounds. If the experience of direction markedly helps people to be open to the living God and to life, then we hope that experience will be allowed to contribute to the Church's understanding of direction and of the whole field of spirituality. If the experience is bad or inconsequential, then we hope it will be recognized as such and replaced by more effective means of helping people to be open to God.

We see this book then as a contribution to a developing spirituality for the contemporary Church. Our aim is to promote the current of Christian spiritual life that runs deeper than short-lived enthusiasms. What we would like most of all is that this book be one voice in a serious ongoing discussion of the experience of spiritual life in the Church, a discussion that we hope will begin not with the question, "What should spirituality be like?" but "What are people's spiritual lives actually like and what has helped to develop them?"

This book has a history of its own. In 1970 the authors, with four other Jesuits, began discussing the possibility of starting a spirituality center in the Boston area. One of us had given retreats and spiritual direction for years and was at that time also engaged in doctoral studies in spiritual theology. The other had finished doctoral studies in clinical psychology and was teaching pastoral counseling and doing spiritual direction at Weston School of Theology. In 1971 we six Jesuits founded the Center for Religious Development in Cambridge, Massachusetts, a center whose threefold purpose is (1) to do research that contributes to the development of a modern spirituality, (2) to train experienced men and women for a more effective ministry of spiritual direction, and (3) to provide spiritual direction to the people of God. While it has tried to be consistently attentive to the achievements of the tradition, the Center staff has based its research, its training, and its service of spiritual direction on personal experience—most fundamentally the experience of both directors and directees with the Mystery we call God. Over the years our spiritual direction has come to be focussed more and more on helping people develop their relationship with God.

As we have come to understand it, spiritual direction differs from moral guidance, psychological counseling, and the practice of confessional, preaching, or healing ministries (though having affinities with them) in that it directly assists individuals in developing and cultivating their personal relationship with God. This understanding, which will be developed at length in the book, has been gradually refined by our experience at the Center for Religious Development and the experience of the many workshops on spiritual direction which we and other staff members have conducted for directors in various parts of the United States, Canada, and other countries.

Since 1971 the staff of the Center for Religious Development has changed to include men and women of varied backgrounds and experience, but through those years the full staff members in particular have helped us beyond measure to keep facing the Mystery and to refine our reflections on the work of spiritual direction. We want to acknowledge the many contributions that have been made to the work of the Center and to this book by all of them: Madeline Birmingham, r.c.;

Robert G. Doherty, S.J.; Anne Harvey, S.N.D.; Evelyn M. Liberatore; Robert E. Lindsay, S.J.; Paul T. Lucey, S.J.; Daniel J. Lusch, S.J.; Joseph F. MacFarlane, S.J.; Joseph E. McCormick, S.J.; and Francine Zeller, O.F.M. We have also been helped by our collaborators on the faculty of Weston School of Theology who have worked with us to develop what is now called the Joint Program in Spiritual Direction.

Whatever worth this book has depends in no small part on the associates who have participated in the training programs in Cambridge. They have come from various backgrounds: priests, sisters, brothers, laymen and laywomen, from the United States, Canada, Japan, the Philippines, New Zealand, Australia, Chile, Jamaica, Ireland, Switzerland, and Germany. We have also helped set up training programs for spiritual directors in Jamaica, Guyana, and Trinidad, again with a variety of directors. All these men and women, who have been willing both to share their desires and struggles to meet the living God and to help others to do the same, have deepened our understanding of the nature of spiritual direction. Some of them have also contributed to this book by offering critiques of the manuscript in its many stages of development.

The quality of the book's contribution to spirituality and to an understanding of spiritual direction is also due to the people who have participated in workshops we have conducted and who have sought spiritual direction at the Center for Religious Development and at other centers in Springfield, Massachusetts; Detroit, Michigan; in Kingston, Jamaica; Port-o-Spain, Trinidad; and Georgetown, Guyana. On any given day the Center in Cambridge might see a Roman Catholic sister working in an inner-city school, a housewife from the suburbs, an Episcopal priest, a cab driver, the wife of a United Church minister, a Methodist professor at a divinity school, and divinity students from any one of the nine theological schools in the Boston Theological Institute. The variety and the quality of the lives of these Christians has increased our confidence in the kind of direction we espouse in this book. We acknowledge with gratitude and a sense of immense privilege all those who have been willing to talk to us about their search for a deeper relationship with God.

We are both members of the Society of Jesus and have, therefore, been strongly influenced by the spirituality of Ignatius of Loyola and his *Spiritual Exercises*. In the history of spirituality, the Exercises of Ignatius would be seen as an example of the kataphatic way of prayer, the way that draws on images, concepts, and reason, as distinct from the apophatic way, which does not depend on images and concepts. Our use of the word "contemplative" will have more affinities with the kataphatic way of prayer. The kind of direction we espouse, however, is not tied to any particular kind of prayer or way. The only prerequisite for engaging in the type of direction we describe is that the person being directed have affective experiences of God which he notices and which he can talk about with a director. Whether these experiences come through centering prayer, the rosary, Ignatian contemplation, dreams, Zen meditation, or any other method of prayer matters little. When a person has such experience, he has the "foodstuff" for spiritual direction as we conceive it, no matter what its source. At the same time we gratefully acknowledge our Ignatian roots and wish to thank our Jesuit brothers who have helped us to appropriate this spirituality.

Over the years various people have translated our scrawl to legible pages as draft succeeded draft. Such translation has often been a labor of love. We are grateful to Catherine Pierni, Mary Street, Ann Freitas, and Evelyn M. Liberatore for devotion that has gone well beyond obligation. We give special thanks to Patricia McCarney, C.N.D., who gave hours of her time and ingenuity to tracking down references and proofreading the manuscript. To Evelyn Liberatore, moreover, we owe so much more. She has been the person who first welcomes those who come to the Center for Religious Development. Her warm and gentle presence and care have made CRD more like a home than an office building.

Besides staff members of CRD—both full staff and associates—other colleagues, friends, and students have read the manuscript in its various versions and have commented helpfully on it. We are grateful to John and Denise Carmody who read it carefully and critically and gave us written critiques; to Daniel Harrington, S.J., who read the first and last version and encouraged us to go on; to the Master of Divinity students and special students who participated in PT366: Spiritual Direction, at Weston School of Theology in 1977 and 1978 and read and commented on the first draft. William A. Barry is especially grateful to Weston School of Theology and the Association of Theological Schools who made possible a sabbatical leave in 1975–76 for research and writing and to Patricia Y. Geoghegan who encouraged him to keep writing and read critically the first drafts of some chapters.

Much of this book was first written at Seabrook Beach, New Hampshire, at the home of Daniel Connolly and John and Margaret Coady, Bill Connolly's uncle and cousins. The graciousness with which they have invited us into their house deserves our deep gratitude and the gratitude of all who have benefited from the time spent and the work done there. If there is in the book any sense of spaciousness, it is due in large part to them and their house on the Atlantic. Eugene and Sally Connolly continued this family graciousness by loaning us their house in New Hampshire for a week of rewriting.

Finally, in the last stages we have been greatly helped by Avery Brooke and Francis Tiso of Seabury Press who have understood what we wanted to communicate, have believed in it, and have helped us to communicate it better.

In the course of the book we frequently use examples to illustrate what we mean. The examples are based on our experience and that of others. Most often they are fictionalized accounts that reflect the experience of a number of people. Sometimes they correspond rather closely to the experience of individuals or a group. In all cases we have changed details of gender, age, place, or topic of conversation to conceal the identity of any individual concerned.

PART ONE

Introducing
Spiritual Direction

What Is Spiritual Direction?

A twenty-four-year-old man approaches a priest and says that he is troubled by a vague uneasiness about the course of his life. Successful in a satisfying job, he enjoys a vibrant social life, has a number of close friends, and is in love with a young woman who reciprocates his love. During his college years he gave up religious practice; but now he finds attendance at the liturgy and participation in a particular liturgical community very rewarding. He is, however, uneasy. Is it possible that he has a vocation to the priesthood? What can the priest do for him?

A married woman of forty attends a talk on prayer and then approaches the pastor who gave it. The woman has two children, ages ten and eight. Her husband works for the telephone company. She finds herself more and more irritable with her husband and children. She feels hemmed in and resentful. She and her husband have joined a couples' group at their church."But God still feels so far away," she says. What can the pastor say to her?

A forty-five-year-old sister makes an opportunity for a conversation with another sister who has a reputation as an able retreat director. She enjoys her work as a high school teacher and likes her community. "I keep hearing sisters talk about prayer," she says, "and I don't know what to make of it. It seems to mean so much to them. Are they exaggerating? I've always prayed regularly, but it's been a duty. Am I missing out on something?" What can the other sister say to her?

A priest about forty years old asks another priest for some help. He feels he has a vocational crisis. He doesn't pray much any more, nor does he get any satisfaction from preaching and presiding at the liturgy. He feels lonely most of the time. Recently he met a widow of thirty-five and found her very attractive. Now he finds himself thinking about her a great deal and wanting to be with her whenever he is not occupied with parish duties. He wants help. What can the other priest say to him?

A married businessman of fifty approaches his minister after church and asks to talk. He is successful, has a good marriage and family, and is a devout Christian. Lately, he says, he has been troubled by the "worldliness" of his life style and by the ethical implications of some of his business dealings. After some discussion it becomes clear that he is concerned about the will of God for himself and about the quality of his relationship with God. How can the minister help him?

A thirty-five-year-old divorcée stops by her neighbor's house. She says she'd like to talk. She has noticed that her neighbor regularly goes to church and that a number of people seem to trust her a lot. This has given her the courage to confide in her. The divorced woman reveals that she has a crippling disease that will gradually incapacitate her. She feels that God is punishing her for her sins, and yet she thinks God is unfair and unjust. "I'm angry at him," she says, "and that makes me feel even more guilty." How can her neighbor help her?

These are only a few examples of the people who approach other Christians for help. Those they approach will respond in a variety of ways.

One could ask for more information and try to help the person understand the causes of his or her malaise. Understanding is usually helpful. One could merely listen sympathetically and offer what little encouragement one can to another human being in pain. Sympathetic listening is very helpful to someone who is troubled. One could help a person see what the consequences of his state in life are and how those consequences might dictate a course of action. One could help another understand that God is not a harsh task-master, but a loving Father, and this theological clarification might be enlightening. One could refer the person to someone else with more knowledge or skill. All of these ways of proceeding could be helpful to the people who have just been described, and all of them could be called pastoral care. *They could not, however, be called spiritual direction.* Instead, spiritual direction is concerned with helping a person directly with his or her relationship with God. It may well be that in each of the human problems mentioned earlier the most fundamental issue is that relationship and its underlying questions: "Who is God for me, and who am I for him?"

Even among spiritual directors, however, we may not find agreement on the kind of help that would be most useful for these people. Various approaches are possible. Let us look at a few.

The neighbor of the divorced woman might undertake a careful explanation to help her realize that God is a forgiving and loving Father, that her illness does not have to be seen as punishment for sins, but one of the sufferings that all humans must expect. The sick woman might benefit a great deal from realizing that her conception of God is not the only possible one for a Christian.

The priest in the first example might ask questions about the young man's past and present way of life, his view of God, his freedom to choose the priesthood, his health. He might ask how the question of a possible vocation to the priesthood arose. Then he might suggest that the young man call the vocation director and perhaps visit the seminary and ask God's help to choose his will. If asked directly, he might well say whether he thought that the signs of a vocation were present or not.

The married woman who feels distant from God might be told that God sometimes maintains distance as a way of testing us and also of helping us recognize our need of him. Her desire for more closeness may indicate that this is what is happening. She can be sure that God will not abandon her if she is faithful to him.

The priest in vocational crisis might be questioned about his practice of prayer and daily liturgy and be counseled to get back to his practices of piety. He could also be advised to join a group of priests who gather regularly for prayer, discussion, and recreation. He might be told that every priest at his age goes through some kind of crisis and that it is at times like this that he needs to be most faithful to his commitments to God.

It is fair to say that the kind of help described in these examples has been the prevailing mode of spiritual direction. A glance at the traditional manuals and many of the articles written on spiritual direction will bear out this assertion.[1] The stress in much of the literature has been on the norms and typical practices of the spiritual life. It must also be fairly stated that such spiritual direction has been and is helpful to people, especially if the director is a good and kind listener, experienced and knowledgeable.

Some questions, however, remain. How does the young man react to the God who may be calling him to priesthood? Does he feel submissive? Passive? Rebellious? How can he address God if he has any of these reactions? And can he expect God to respond to his reactions?

How does the priest react to the God to whom he is committed? How can he express his reactions? What can happen if he does?

How does the married woman who feels distance from God address him? Does she tell him that she knows he knows best? Even if she is not sure that he either knows or cares?

These and similar questions point to another kind of help. The ministering person helps the other to address God directly and to listen to what God has to communicate. The focus of this kind of spiritual direction is the relationship itself between God and the person. The person is helped not so much to understand that relationship better, but to engage in it, to enter into dialogue with God. Spiritual direction of this kind focusses on what happens when a person listens to and responds to a self-communicating God.

Thus, the young man who is nagged by the thought of a possible vocation to the priesthood can be helped to develop a more personal relationship with God in prayer on the assumption that God and he can work out together whether God does have a special call for him and how he may want to respond to that call.

The married woman can be helped to voice her desire for a closer relationship to the God who can respond to that desire.

The priest with the vocational crisis might be helped to discover whether he wants a closer relationship with God and if so, how to approach God with such a desire. He might put his concerns before God, express his deepest hopes, fears, disappointments to God in prayer, and pay attention to God's communication with him. The decision about his life goals would then come in the context of the ensuing relationship.

The businessman can begin to look at what his "troubles" about life style mean, whether he is looking for something more in his relationship with God, and then he might enter into dialogue with God about his desires for God and God's desires for him. The divorced woman can be helped to tell God directly how she feels, how ambivalent she is, and to listen to his response.

Once these people have begun to listen to God and to tell him how listening to him affects them, then they may want continued help with the ensuing dialogue and relationship; that is, they may want ongoing spiritual direction. The purpose of this book is to assist ministering persons in offering ongoing spiritual direction of this type more competently and confidently to those who are looking for it.

Spiritual direction, as we understand it then, is directly concerned with a person's actual experiences of his relationship with God. There have recently been frequent allusions among spiritual directors to "kinds" or "models" of direction.[2] We suggest that the basic issue is not so much whether there should be different kinds of spiritual direction, but rather what focus is proper to direction. To establish religious experience (insofar as that experience is expressive of one's relationship to God) as the focus of direction does not seem a more or less arbitrary adoption of a particular kind or model of direction. It seems, rather, an attempt to identify the question that is most basic to direction and to let the direction take shape around that question.

For us, therefore, religious experience is to spiritual direction what foodstuff is to cooking. Without foodstuff there can be no cooking. Without religious experience there can be no spiritual direction.

We define Christian spiritual direction, then, as help given by one Christian to another which enables that person to pay attention to God's personal communication to him or her, to respond to this personally communicating God, to grow in intimacy with this God, and to live out the consequences of the relationship. The *focus* of this type of spiritual direction is on experience, not ideas, and specifically on religious experience, i.e., any experience of the mysterious Other whom we call God.[3] Moreover, this experience is viewed, not as an isolated event, but as an expression of the ongoing personal relationship God has established with each one of us.

Spiritual direction has always aimed ultimately at fostering union with God and has, therefore, had to do with the individual's relationship with God. At the same time it is fair to say that in our lifetime, at least, the focus of most spiritual directors has not been as clearly on the experience of the relationship with God as we describe it here. For the present it is enough to underline the fact that our view of spiritual direction puts primary focus on experiences of God, most often occurring in prayer. The spiritual director is most interested in what happens when a person consciously puts himself into the presence of God. Not that the director has little or no interest in the rest of a person's life. He is interested in the whole person, but the focus of interest is the prayer experience of the directee.

"Spiritual direction" is one of the more grandiloquent terms church ministry has inherited from the past. In our cultural environment it also is one of the most confusing. This confusion may be best expressed by an image.

When one hears someone described as a spiritual director, one might, at least subconsciously, picture an ageless, emaciated man in a cowled robe, with his eyes cast down and his hands hidden in flowing sleeves. He sits in a whitewashed, cramped room with one small, barred window high on the wall beside him. Opposite him, wearing dun-colored traveling-dress and bonnet, sits a seventeenth-century French lady. Between them is a table on which rest a skull and a guttered candle. She is describing the miseries of managing the family estate with her husband away at Court for much of the year. He is murmuring about being alone with the Alone, or dictating an horarium that will enable her to bring a measure of monastic order and piety into her life.

The image is not, of course, original. Most readers will recognize its elements. It is useful, not because it is attractive or historically accurate, but because, as caricatures will, it sums up, magnifies, and focusses many of the attitudes modern men and women—both Catholic and Protestant—have toward spiritual direction—when they know anything about it at all. It smells of an archaic, hierarchic social and religious system in which a person could be told how to live, and in detail.[4] It suggests a distaste for life and withdrawal from it, a ponderous, intricate system of thought that makes no contact with the basic energies and drives of life, but always floats a little above them, like a cloud-world. It intimates bored, empty people searching for "enriching" experiences and contemplative clergymen hypnotized by the adulation of the *haut monde*. Its atmosphere is charged with unquestioned male domination.

Much of the difficulty, of course, is caused by the term itself. In our culture "religious" sounds alien enough, but "spiritual" can rub raw our sensitivity to the precious and the artificial, and connote thought and behavior that cannot survive contact with earth and full sun. For socially aware Christians it can suggest a preoccupation with introspection, with turning one's mental gaze in on one's own emotional and moral life rather than outward to the world where people are in need and the peace and justice of the Kingdom must be advocated.

"Direction," the activity of directing someone, or the experience of being directed by someone, is similarly alien to contemporary culture, suggesting as it does the rejection of personal responsibility and the acceptance of the authority of the one who does the directing.

Thus, the term "spiritual direction" unavoidably suggests to people of our contemporary Western culture a spiritualism and an authoritarianism that sound theology and psychology must repudiate. We must remember that in all aspects of his life the human being can only act as body-spirit, and any help toward personal development that overlooks this fact is likely to be more harmful than helpful to him. In the same way, sound "direction" cannot mean that one gives responsibility for his life to someone else. "My director told me to do it" can never justify a course of action. The person who receives direction must always retain personal responsibility, and the mode and content of sound direction will help him to retain and develop personal responsibility, not make it more difficult for him to do so.

Yet the term also has its uses. "Spiritual" does tell us that the basic concern of this kind of help is not with external actions as such, but with the inner life, the "heart," the personal core out of which come the good and evil that people think and do. It includes "head," but points to more than reason and more than knowledge. It also reminds us that another Spirit, the spirit of the Lord, is involved. "Direction" does suggest something more than advice-giving and problem-solving. It implies that the person who seeks direction is going somewhere, and wants to talk to someone on the way. It implies, too, that the talk will not be casual and aimless, but apt to help him find his way.

So, although the term is liable to misunderstanding, it is probably more descriptive of the experience it points to than "religious counseling," "spiritual counseling," or "spiritual advice." It is, besides, firmly entrenched in the tradition and is more widely and spontaneously used than any term that has been proposed to replace it.

With some misgivings, therefore, we continue to use the term spiritual direction. We hope that the book will dispel some of the confusion surrounding the term and put to rest most of the fears emanating from the caricature.

The other terms mentioned and discarded as less appropriate do, however, indicate the realm of pastoral care within which spiritual direction as we practice it resides. This type of spiritual direction is generally one-to-one; the relationship between director and directed is a helping one, and it is entered upon, as we shall see, on a quasi-contractual basis. Just as pastoral counseling may focus on the marital relationship, so this form focusses on the relationship with God. Indeed, spiritual direction may be considered the core form from which all other forms of pastoral care radiate, since ultimately all forms of pastoral care and counseling aim, or should aim, at helping people to center their lives in the mystery we call God.

Like other areas of pastoral ministry, spiritual direction is exercised not only by ministers who have a specialized interest in this area, but also by others who are equally engaged in a number of other areas of ministry. We hope this book can be a help to all of them, but our focus will be on those who specialize in this work. We do not intend to provide techniques or charts or methods, but to help persons become spiritual directors. The reader who expects a treatise on the spiritual life with its practices and stages of development will be disappointed, as will the reader who hopes for a systematic theological treatment of spiritual direction. We will concentrate on processes: the process of developing a relationship with God, the process of helping another to relate consciously to God and to grow in that relationship, and the process of becoming a spiritual director. Since our aim is not simply to increase a person's knowledge, but to help him or her become someone, namely a spiritual director, the book will probably be of most help to those who discuss it and their own work in groups, especially in supervisory groups of some kind. Becoming someone occurs most effectively through relationships with others.

2

The Centrality
of Religious Experience

The various persons approached by others in need in the examples in the first chapter might well experience a sense of panic at the thought that they are being asked to give spiritual direction. Many of our readers may be saying "Who? Me?" and perhaps even recalling the feelings of inadequacy that surged in them when someone asked them for help with prayer. Such feelings of inadequacy to the task of aiding others in their prayer life have probably always been an initial, and appropriate, reaction to the request, "Teach me to pray!," no matter how that request was phrased. The man or woman who would lightly take on such a task is probably not to be trusted. But modern ministers may have even more reason to feel inadequate. We are part of a cultural shift of massive proportions. We have all witnessed the loss of credibility of many of the institutions, agencies, customs, and theories upon which we all counted, often without even knowing it, for the guarantee of our view of reality and of right and wrong. When so much has changed, we can wonder indeed whether we do have anything to offer to those who seek help with prayer and the central question of the meaning of their lives.

Our first task in this chapter is to try to understand the cultural and religious context in which we work as spiritual directors. It would be wise and even salutary for us to recall where we were before the tumult of the sixties. Most of us accepted without question the integrity of our political leaders and agreed with the rightness of our national purpose. Capitalism, with its free enterprise and strong labor union movement, was accepted as the system most hospitable to the ideals of our democratic way of life. We are not here harking back to the "good old days" as "praisers of past times." We are trying to evoke for our readers a sense of what a difference the sixties and seventies have made in our world view. Many social and political attitudes we took for granted before the sixties we now question or even discard as hopelessly naive. These changes in attitude toward our social and cultural institutions and values have deeply affected all of us and have contributed to the feelings of inadequacy and doubt that many clergy experience.

Roman Catholics, of course, have experienced another revolution. Before the sixties the Roman Catholic Church seemed impervious to change. Nor, in the minds of most Catholics, did it need much change. Seminaries and religious congregations were crowded. Across the country large buildings were erected at great cost to take care of the expected continued influx of novices and seminarians. Church attendance was high. New churches and schools were being built at a rapid rate. The authority of the Pope, bishops, and priests was relatively unquestioned. Catholics knew who they were and how they were expected to behave, and if they did not behave as expected, they knew they had sinned and went to confession. That time and many of those attitudes disappeared after the changes of the Second Vatican Council and the turmoil of the sixties and seventies. No doubt, Christians in other churches can document similar institutional upheavals. It is apparent that, for better or worse, we are in a new situation.

Until very recent times, seminaries and divinity schools gave short shrift to developing the focus and skills of spiritual direction. Spirituality and spiritual direction were peripheral to the main business of seminary education. At most a minor course was offered in ascetical and mystical theology or in prayer. Few, if any, programs existed whose purpose was to enable future priests and ministers to respond to the request, "Teach me to pray." Many clergy today face with dismay and feelings of inadequacy the increasing demand for help with prayer because we have had no training for this work. We recognize that little in our past experience or training has prepared us for what people now seem to need.

The cultural shift which shakes our sense of ministerial adequacy also, we believe, creates the demand for spiritual direction. When social and religious institutions and values are shared by most people and seem to be working reasonably well, values and meaning tend to be mediated by the institutions and the cultural, social, and familial environment in which individuals are reared. Only the occasional maverick or gadfly raises questions about the system itself. Most of us take our values for granted and do not recognize that they rest upon assumptions that are not absolute truths. When, for example, "everyone" is a believer, there is no necessity for most people to ground their belief in critical reflection on their own experience; belief is taken for granted. What happens, however, when institutions begin to break down? Then the web of assumptions they helped to form begins to tear, and many people feel themselves adrift in a chaotic and increasingly senseless world. They search for some way to make sense out of life or at least to ease the pain.

And so we have witnessed the rise of all sorts of movements that seem to promise some way to find meaning in life. Psychotherapy and counseling are sought, not just for help with neurosis or with career choices, but for help with living in a world whose center does not seem to hold. Encounter groups, growth groups, experience groups, and others have become popular as people strive to find community and meaning. There has been a phenomenal growth of interest in the religious practices of the East, and cult groups have spread rapidly. In the established churches we have seen a rise of interest in prayer and in the gifts of the Spirit. Retreats of all kinds have flourished. Spiritual directors find it difficult to keep up with the demand for their services.

This search for meaning, for a rock that will give stability in a rapidly changing world, is, at root, a religious quest. Times of social and cultural upheaval seem to set people off on a search for a radical security. What they most want are guides who will lead them to that security, and priests, ministers, and other religious leaders often seem the likely candidates for the job. Hence the increased requests for pastoral counseling and spiritual direction. But requests are often addressed to guides who feel that they do not know the way themselves. In biblical terms, the sheep find that there are no shepherds.

This situation poses severe dangers. We can see in our culture that gurus who promise answers can have a mesmerizing effect on many people. It may be that interminable psychotherapy is for many a solution to their uncertainty.[1] We have seen instances where spiritual directors became the solution—with traumatic results when the directors betrayed their feet of clay. In another time of social, cultural, and religious upheaval Thomas More addressed a similar situation. While he was in prison, his daughter Margaret asked him whether he had been influenced by Cardinal John Fisher to refuse the oath of supremacy. After much praise of Fisher, More replied: "Verily, daughter, I never intend (God being my good Lord) to pin my soul at another man's back, not even the best man that I know this day living: for I know not whither he may hap to carry it. There is no man living, of whom while he liveth, I may make myself sure."[2] But if we who are religious leaders are ourselves uncertain, where shall we turn? What can we trust as rock? To what do we pin our souls? In the following pages we shall endeavor to demonstrate that it is possible to find such a rock and help others to find that rock. The rock is not any other human being, but the mystery we call God, as that mystery is experienced in each person's own heart and mind and spirit.

Whether we are approached by someone searching for something that will give meaning to a life that seems adrift, or by someone who explicitly wants to develop a stronger and more personal relationship with God, we are faced with the same question: Where to begin? In both instances the request would not have been made if accepted ways and objective truths had not somehow been found wanting. These requests force us to ask fundamental questions: Do we believe in a God who actually does communicate with his people both corporately and as individuals? Do we believe that he can be met personally and that relationship with him can ground an individual's life on rock? If we do believe these things, where do people meet this God? Ultimately, we believe, each person meets God in his or her own experience whether that experience occurs with a community at a liturgical or paraliturgical service, or with one or two others, or alone.

For better or worse, in our world at any rate, each person can only find a rock that will not give way or shatter by answering the question: In my own experience do I meet a mysterious Other to whom I can say: You are the Rock of my salvation? In the modern world where unbelief has become or is rapidly becoming "the natural or normative condition,"[3] believers have two options. One is to retreat into smaller and smaller ghettos of "true believers" who reinforce one another's "beleaguered faith." The other is to go to the heart of Christianity. That heart is the experience in faith, hope, and love that Jesus is my savior and the world's and that I want to respond to him; in other words, that heart is prayer and life based on prayer.[4] The first option ultimately means that the Christian pins his soul at the back of the other "true believers" and not at the back of God. Moreover, he tends to retreat from any mission to the world. The only serious Christian option is, we believe, the second. In the present sociological conditions of a pluralistic society in which belief is only one option among others, the rock upon which we stand cannot ultimately be anyone else's experience; it has to be our own. We have too often experienced the fragility of "another man's back."

This position, however, must not be taken to mean that each of us is a monad uninfluenced by others. Christians, by definition, are a people, a community of believers who influence one another's faith and experience and life. And Christians rest their faith on authority: the authority of the Bible, of the Church Fathers, of the Councils, of the various credal statements, of the hierarchy of their churches. But Christians have always been asked to appropriate what authority states, to make it their own, to say "*I* believe." In times of cultural upheaval the need for such personal appropriation is more compelling.

But if we are thrown back upon our own experience, are we not faced with an impossible situation? Psychoanalysis has shown us the seeming impossibility of knowing ourselves enough to be sure that we are not deluding ourselves. All our experience is structured and the structures we use are the products of our past experiences; we cannot have a "pure" experience unaffected by the structures of our own personalities and minds. How can we be sure that our "experiences of God" are really "of God," and not "of ourselves?"[5] The sociology of knowledge raises a similar and perhaps more difficult question with its insight into the mindsets produced by the societies and cultures and institutions to which we belong.[6] Admittedly, both the psychoanalytic critique and the sociology of knowledge can also be turned on those who profess unbelief, but turning the tables does no more than establish that both believers and unbelievers seemingly are without clothes. The question still remains: How can I, on the basis of my experience, say with assurance that I believe in a God who does exist and who in Jesus Christ has touched my life at its core?

A number of modern thinkers provide a first approximation of an answer. Peter Berger is one example. While it is true, he says, that "nothing is immune to the relativization of socio-cultural analysis,"[7] God is not thereby proved nonexistent. He then suggests that theology begin not with the God who reveals, but with the human being and his human experience. In other words, Berger says that the very human experience which is in question is paradoxically the place where we will find an answer. There, and there only, will we find the "signals of transcendence," the "rumor of angels."

Any serious inquiry into human experience will reveal a rumor of angels, says Berger. How do we then decide whether the rumor is really of angels or not? Does the reality of which we have signals really exist? Thus, attention to human experience faces us with the question of God. The question is not answered merely by being asked. Neither can it be dismissed as frivolous. The effort to answer it requires a turn to interiority since the answer is arrived at not by examining some external instance or object, but by coming to terms with the full implications of what it means to be an asker of the question. Berger's conclusions are consonant with those of the transcendental method which undergirds the theology of such eminent theologians as Karl Rahner[8] and Bernard Lonergan.[9] Ultimately the inquiring subject comes to the judgment that the existence of God is the a priori possibility for his own existence as an inquiring subject. However, no one but the inquiring subject can make this judgment for himself, and to do this he needs to take seriously his own inner experience and operations. The search for a rock upon which we could ground our search for meaning has led us to the realization that attention to inner experience, a continuing concern of spiritual theology and spiritual direction, is of central importance.

A person may be helped to acknowledge the existence of God by attending to his own experience. Can he, however, come to the belief that this God has come close and is communicating himself? "Does this God care for me?" "Has he saved me?" These are the existential questions people are asking. How do we help people answer such questions? Again, recourse has to be made to the experience of the individual. My experience is influenced by the environment I grew up in, the church I belong to, the teaching and witness I have been exposed to. But ultimately I have to say: I believe that Jesus is my savior; I believe that I have been grasped by his love and have experienced that love in faith. No one else's experience and faith will do. This is the rock upon which I can stand with faith-ful assurance that it will not crumble. We who are asked to teach people to pray must be able to help them come to this assurance by giving God a chance to demonstrate his care and concern to them and by helping them to pay attention to their inner experience when they give him this chance.

Our reflections on the modern context of the request, "Teach me to pray," have led us to the conclusion that our best approach to offering such help is to concentrate on the religious experience of the one who seeks the help. We hope that these reflections have removed some of the anxiety that our readers experience as they enter upon the ministry of spiritual direction. We do not need elaborate techniques. We do not have to be "holy" in some otherworldly sense. We do need some biblical and theological knowledge. But most of all, we need an interest in and a willingness to explore religious experience with those who seek us out, uncovering together the relationship which this experience is revealing.

It may be helpful to point out that theology itself is undergoing a radical shift to interiority, a paradigm shift[10] of enormous impact. Bernard Lonergan in *Method in Theology* [11] has shown that the transcendental method, such as we touched on in following Berger, supplies only one component for theological method. It enables a person to know and affirm himself as a being whose basic dynamism is toward self-transcendence in knowledge and love, as a being on the lookout for God. Theological method, however, also needs a religious component, needs to know that God has actually spoken, has communicated himself in knowledge and love.

Lonergan makes the paradigm shift from objectivity to interiority or intersubjectivity in a bold stroke; for him the religious component is provided by experience, the experience of being in love with God. Transcendental method demonstrates that I am a being with the capacity for self-transcendence. The religious component is supplied when I can say that this capacity has been actualized, that is, that God is in love with me and I with him.

Thus, Lonergan's theological method grounds itself not on deductions from some set of first propositions, but on religious experience, the experience of being in love with God. It is grounded on the answer to this question: Do I experience in some dim fashion the fulfillment of my deepest desires and hopes?

In his chapter on the foundations of theology Lonergan makes clear that the foundations for systematic and pastoral theology are not premises, but converted people, including converted theologians. Thus, theology, a discipline that for so long a time[12] had little to do with religious experience, now finds itself thrust back upon such experience for its very foundations. Spiritual directors and other pastoral workers who have found themselves forced to focus on religious experience in order to help people are finding that theologians are adopting the same focus. A new age of mutual collaboration which will heal the rift between dogmatic or school theology and spirituality may well be upon us.

The focus on religious experience which we see as helpful, and even necessary, for spiritual growth in our time is not a new phenomenon in the history of spirituality. It is as old as Christianity itself. From earliest times dedicated Christians have grounded their lives on their experience of God and the conscious relationship which developed from attention to that experience. The literature that reflects the belief and practice of the Christian people at different points in their history often encourages the acceptance of religious experience and of the dialogical life that can develop from it.

The apostles came to believe in Jesus and to trust in him through their experience of him. A great deal of thought about Jesus has resulted from their experience, but the basis for the thought was experience itself. A look at the New Testament makes this point clear.

All the gospels describe the disciples as men who did not begin their relationship with Jesus with a preconceived picture of him that was later substantiated. They came to know him, they observed him, joined his company, watched the way he acted, and listened to him speak. Their experience of him led them to raise questions about him and then enabled them to answer those questions. They saw him touch a leper before he healed him, speak words of forgiveness to the paralyzed man, challenge the Pharisees to say whether they wanted him to kill or give life on the Sabbath, respond with sympathy and power to the widow of Naim, invite the hemorrhaging woman to speak to him. They experienced him in these actions and many others. And their conviction about him and allegiance to him resulted from their experience.

The gospels indicate a development in the apostles' attitude toward Jesus. They first see him as a person of power and only later come to accept him as the Messiah. They are depicted as reacting with horror to his initial descriptions of how his Messiahship would be lived out. Only after the resurrection do they come to recognize his betrayal and death as the way God was willing to have salvation achieved. Thus the disciples are described as men in the process of experiencing and of developing conviction on the basis of that experience. Christianity rests on that bedrock.

When Athanasius[13] described the spiritual journey of Antony the Hermit, he spoke of him as beginning his journey not because he came to a conclusion based on sound thought but because he heard the gospel proclaimed to him. He heard the words of Jesus, "If you would be perfect, go, sell what you possess and give to the poor, and you will have treasure in heaven; and come, follow me," as words addressed to him; he reacted to them and decided to respond with acceptance. Athanasius saw the proclamation of the gospel and Antony's response to it as an experience and wanted to tell his readers that the life of Antony and the development of his virtues and charisms were based on this as well as on other experiences.

Early Christian literature contains many other such incidents. Preachers and writers had the expectation that God would deal with people as he was' shown dealing with them in the Bible.[14] The experience of dialogue with God did not, for them, cease with the ascension of Jesus, but rather continued in the experience of people who lived the life of the Church.

Clement of Alexandria[15] described Christian life in terms of the Word acting as companion educator (*paidagogos*) of the Christian person. The paidagogos in Hellenistic culture was a family servant who from a child's early years took him in charge, accompanied him to school through the sometimes perilous city streets, was with him as he made his way in a bustling city, and through his example, advice, and the decisions he made helped him learn to live in his environment.[16] His task was not primarily academic. The schoolmaster taught the child his school subjects. The paidagogos, who spent much of the day with him, helped him learn through the companionship itself. To Clement's mind the Word, Christ, does this for us. The servant and the child formed a relationship that drew on the affective resources of both. The same would take place in the relationship between Christ and the Christian person. In this relationship the person could grow toward maturity in his relationship with God and with life.[17] This way of seeing a Christian's growth is readily open to an understanding that a continuing dialogue takes place between Christ and the Christian person and that the dialogue occurs in shifting circumstances and continues through stages of development. In anyone's life, dialogue with another person close to him changes as both people grow. Clement's image of Christian life encourages us to assume that the same will be true of the relationship with Christ.

In another work written by an unknown author at about the same time, the *To Diognetus*,[18] a person's conversion from paganism takes place through coming to know the Father who has loved human beings and has invited them to love him. It is this coming to know and love him who "has first loved you" that serves as the basis for Christian life. The person learns how to live from the God who has loved him. His growth as a Christian is described not in terms of his conformity or nonconformity to laws, but in terms of his becoming more like the God who has met him. He ceases to be a person who makes self-centered use of his power and wealth and becomes a person who takes on himself other people's burdens. His experience of God and Christian life will lead him gradually into the deeper recesses of the mystery of God's relationship with us.

In both these works the description of Christian life encourages us to look on our lives as relationships between God and ourselves, relationships that require mutual communication. God speaks to us in both word and action, and we have the ability to respond. This way of seeing his Christian life was facilitated for the Christian by the way in which Scripture was delivered to him by the Church. Scripture was proclaimed at liturgical services. The Bible was not a book meant for silent, private reading. Even outside the liturgy it was read aloud by a servant or read aloud by oneself. This context in which the word of God was heard did not prevent people from thinking about it. Thought about the Scripture was highly encouraged; the context itself, however, was not that of private study but of announcement by one person to another that brought about reaction and a response either of withdrawal or nearer approach to God.

The word was addressed to the whole people, but it was also addressed to the individual. The homilist not only spoke of the pertinence of the word to the people of God but showed his audience that the word was meant to address the individual life, the circumstances in which that life was lived, and the development that would take place in it. The "moral sense" or "spiritual sense" declared that God had each individual's life in mind when he spoke his word. God spoke, the person reacted and then decided on his response. Life could thus be readily seen as a dialogue of both word and action between God and ourselves. The scriptural appeals to the heart prevented the dialogue from becoming purely rational. The liturgical setting, in which the Scriptures were delivered to the community, itself encouraged people to listen with their hearts and their feelings as well as with their minds.

For a thousand years liturgical services presented God as speaking to his people and calling for reaction and response from them. The affective hearing of the word would itself be an experience closer to what we mean by religious experience than our customary silent reading of Scripture would be. And closer, too, than the discussion of the word of God that in most recent centuries became the substance of homilies and sermons. For us to speak then of religious experience as basic to Christian life and prayer does not mean that we are proposing a new basis for prayer. It seems rather to mean that we are pointing to an element that has been, from the beginning, at the heart of the Christian tradition.[19]

It is also clear that dialogue with the word of God in Scripture is natural to Christian prayer. Twelfth-century Aelred of Rievaulx in his *When Jesus Was Twelve Years Old*,[20] moves spontaneously from describing Jesus' adventure in the temple to speaking directly to him. In doing this he exemplifies receptivity to the word for the person he is writing to. He also shows us how a person can spontaneously react to the word of God.

Medieval writers found the dialogue of spiritual life dramatically exemplified in the *Song of Songs*.[21] William of St. Thierry in his *Exposition of the Song of Songs*,[22] for example, sees the Bridegroom initiating the spiritual life as a life of relationship with himself. The Bride responds to his initiative. The development of the relationship between them takes place because he desires relationship with her and she desires relationship with him. There are verbal dialogues in the *Song*, but principally the dialogue is seen as one of action. One person's actions communicate to the other person. The other person then decides whether to respond or not. The *Exposition* considers the pauses, disappearances, and hesitations of the Son as descriptions of Christian life. The process contains moments of frustration, of unfulfilled hope, of seeking in darkness. But throughout the *Exposition* the desire of Bride and Bridegroom to relate to one another is a continuing and sustaining current.

William, like other medieval writers, had a high respect for knowledge. He respects the fact that intellect knows. However, he believes that love knows too, and that finally the person knows God through loving him. The use of the relationship of Bride and Bridegroom as the image of developing spiritual life makes it easy to understand the centrality of experience as a writer like William understood it. Rational knowledge has a distinguished place in his understanding of spiritual life. But it is love based on experience that reaches God.[23]

Writers like William believed in institutions. The Church, secular society, the monastic foundation were of supreme importance to them and provided the setting of their lives of personal encounter with God. But these were not themselves that encounter. The encounter took place in their relationship with God. It required an awareness of God's love and an awareness of his personal call to receive that love and respond to it. The response could carry the person to uncharted, unthinkable places but it was always a response to a word that had been spoken and continued to be spoken in the person's heart.

Spirituality at the end of the Middle Ages shows many signs of the conflict between the emphasis on rational knowledge of God and the emphasis on loving experience of God.[24] Ignatius of Loyola, as a late medieval person, had a choice between these different emphases. His works[25] show that he chose to put trust in his experience. He had ardent respect for the authority of the Church, despite considerable suffering at the hands of some of the people who wielded it, and he never questioned its claim on him. Authority, however, did not substitute for the communication that God could address to an individual heart and the response that the person could make.[26] His life became a dialogue between God calling and sustaining him and Ignatius responding. He was willing to choose untravelled roads because he knew that God would lead and sustain him along those roads.

These are indications of how Christian tradition through the centuries has been open to the individual's experience of God and has encouraged dialogical relationship which can result from that experience. It is appropriate that our final example be Ignatius of Loyola. His *Spiritual Exercises*, based on the conviction that God can and wants to be met in dialogue, have for many generations exemplified the Christian tradition's acceptance of experience and encouragement of the dialogue with God. The *Exercises* have also expressed for us the conviction that talking about one's experience of that dialogue with a spiritual director can be helpful for the development of the dialogical relationhip.

PART TWO

Fostering the Relationship Between the Directee and the Lord

The Relationship Between God and Individuals

Spiritual direction is help with the development of one's relationship with the Lord. The persons most immediately involved in spiritual direction are the Lord, the directee, and the director. The relationship between director and directee can be crucial for the development of the relationship between the directee and the Lord, but the latter relationship exists prior to and is independent of the former. Directors do not create relationships between God and their directees; they try to foster such relationships.

The Lord is mystery, the wholly Other whom we cannot know or name in any adequate fashion. Our assumption is that he wants to relate to his people both as a community and as individuals. God does not need anyone to help him relate to his people. But the human other does seek help to develop his or her relationship with God. And it is to the person of the directee and to ways of helping him or her grow in the relationship with the Lord that we now turn.

It has been our experience in workshops and training programs on spiritual direction that it is difficult for people to grasp the import of our focus on religious experience and the relationship wtih God. For a time we did not understand what was happening when in the middle of a workshop it became clear that at least some of the participants were hearing us in ways we had not intended. Gradually we came to realize that definition and description did not adequately convey our meaning and that we needed to spend time helping our hearers get a feel for, a taste of what lay behind the concepts "religious experience" and "relationship with God." In this chapter we intend to do the same for our readers. Our purpose is not to define these terms so much as to invite readers to recall their own experiences and to see whether those experiences echo what we describe.

When we talk about the relationship that is expressed and developed in prayer, we immediately encounter a problem of language. Our tendency is to become abstract. To describe a person's difficulties in expressing his fear, for example, to God, we may resort to psychological language and use terms like "affective underdevelopment," "identity issues," "inability to achieve psychic intimacy." Or we may turn to theological categories and speak of the struggle between grace and sin. Both of these modes of explanation may accurately describe the person's situation, but they do not adequately represent what is for the person the most important dimension of all, his concrete relationship with God. To describe this relationship we need another terminology. It must be relational because it describes a relationship, religious because we are talking about the relationship with God, and concrete because we want to talk about the experience of that relationship, not the idea of it.

What do we mean by "relationship with God?" We mean something that *is*, first of all. It is established by the creation of the human person and exists even when the person is unaware of its existence. I am a creature whether I know it or not, and God is my creator. God knows me as his son or daughter even when I do not know him as Father. Jesus knows me as his brother or sister even when I am unaware of this bond. However, any person who does not know his father, his mother, his brothers or sisters suffers from a lack that will probably show itself in some way in his consciousness. He may experience it as rootlessness, or as a sense of being radically alone, or as a sense of being lost. So, too, the lack of awareness of the God who is in relationship with us may show itself in consciousness. The fear of being left alone with all our fears, unfulfilled hopes, and self-doubt is a fear many of us seem to experience at times. Most of us do not express it often, but it influences us nonetheless. The lack may also show itself positively in the yearning some people express of contact with a deeper level of life that they cannot name.

Our faith tells us that God communicates with us whether we know it or not by continuously creating and redeeming us. He shares himself with us even when we do not know that he is doing so. Life itself communicates him to us. The first crocus communicates the indomitability of life. Sunsets tell us of grandeur. Friendship communicates to us the experience of loyalty and love. Blizzards and hurricanes impose on us the consciousness that the ordering of nature is ultimately outside our control. The harnessing of nuclear energy makes us aware that there is no limit to our ability to explore and exploit our universe, and nuclear accidents make us aware that we cannot perfectly control what we have discovered.

In these and many other ways, the Christian acknowledges, God communicates with us. He does so whether we name him as the source of the communication or not. We are being "spoken to" continuously.

When one person communicates with another on a particular occasion—for example, a man leaves a bouquet of roses for a woman he admires—we can speak of an experience of communication. It is an experience of explicit communication on the part of the person who initiates it. It is only an experience of implicit communication for the recipient, however, if he does not know someone is communicating with him. The woman, for example, may delight in the beauty of the roses but assume that they were intended for her sister. When the intended receiver does know, the communication is an experience of explicit communication on his or her part too. A particular religious experience is an experience of explicit communication on both God's and the receiver's part. The person knows that God is communicating with him at this moment.[1]

We remain free, however, to listen to God's communication or not to listen, and free to respond or not to respond to what we hear. When we speak of contemplative prayer, we are speaking at the same time of awareness of this communication by God and of a willingness to listen to him and respond to him. Conscious relationship begins when I choose to listen or to look at what the other is doing. After I have made this choice, I then freely decide whether to respond or not. Thus, by contemplative prayer we mean the conscious willingness and desire to look at and listen to God as he wishes to be for me and to respond to him. I may accept or reject him as he wishes to be. In either case I have responded. When this process occurs, the person has the "foodstuff" for beginning spiritual direction.

A further precision needs to be made. We can speak of any individual religious experience as an expression of God's desire to be in personal relationship with us, a relationship initiated by him and acknowledged and responded to by us. But there can be two different kinds of events that we call religious experience. One is spontaneous and can occur when a person is praying as well as when he is not praying. It brings about a reaction to God and a desire to respond to him in some way. But it seems to end there. A man is walking along a country road in winter at sunset and is struck with awe at the lavish beauty around him. He is elated and shouts aloud a thank you to God. He then goes home and tells his wife about the experience. He recalls the event at times, but it remains a relatively isolated experience of God.

The other kind of event is a similar experience that is not isolated from the fabric of the person's life but begins or is part of an ongoing conscious relationship with God. For instance, the awe at the sunset might remind the man of how much he has taken God for granted lately and prod him to take up again his practice of spending some time each day in prayer to deepen his relationship with God. It is the latter experience that we want to focus on in this chapter because it is this more purposeful pursuit of the relationship with God that makes spiritual direction most profitable.

If you ask people what happens when they pray, you get a variety of answers. Some say it is hard to pray; others say it is easy; still others say it is sometimes difficult, sometimes easy. The fact seems to be that prayer, in general, is neither difficult nor easy. It is no more difficult than the formation of any deep, enduring, trustworthy relationship, and no easier. The comparison is closer than it may at first appear. If you converse with a person for a half hour or more several times a week about personal subjects, you soon find that either a close relationship has developed or that something is wrong between you and the other person. If there is mutual communication and mutual acceptance of hopes, desires, ideals, fears, and frustrations, the relationship cannot be anything but close.

The Old and New Testaments demonstrate the aptness of the comparison. They are a record of God's expression of his attitudes toward us. We see how he lives out his love, his concern, his willingness to be involved with us. These attempts to communicate with us are not the efforts of an academician to make himself clear. Yahweh speaks with tenderness, dismay, anger, concern. Jesus addresses people invitingly, angrily, sadly, ardently, compassionately. God's desire to enter a mutual relationship with us leads to direct confrontations with people that call for a response from them. He calls people by name. He helps them in times of trouble, rescues them from oppression, forgives them their obtuseness and recalcitrance, shows them a mother's love. Jesus weeps for people, struggles to help them understand him, patiently tells them about the Father, warns them, urges them, takes them to task.

Those who set themselves to hear the word, then, meet a God who addresses his own attitudes to them directly. This directness invites his listeners to react. More than that, it may not let them rest until they do react. The gospels, in particular, are written in such a way that they elicit reaction. It is only in terms of this eliciting of reaction that they can be properly understood.

Those who do listen to them tend to react to them as they would to any provocative statements addressed to them. They like or dislike what they hear. They want to hear more or they want to stop listening. If they dislike what they hear and physically cannot avoid hearing, they may try psychically to avoid it by falling into boredom or active antagonism. If they like it, they tend to respond with approval, hope, joy, contentment, or with some appropriate activity.

As response takes place, whether it is approving or disapproving, the God who speaks the word may seem different. He may express attitudes he did not express before the reaction took place. When he is greeted with anger, for instance, he may begin to express a patient attention. When his word encounters acceptance, he may express love. This is the way with the word. It expresses a living Being who wants to engage in dialogue with us. The more explicit and specific the response is, the more readily the dialogue proceeds.

This language of dialogue may seem strange to some of our readers. We are not speaking of "auditions," although they sometimes seem to happen. For most people the word of God comes more subtly and less tangibly, but no less really than this. After a particularly stormy outburst against God, for example, a person might "sense" that God is still there listening patiently, wondering if there is any more the person has to say. Or, after a person has over and over confessed unworthiness, the thought may come unexpectedly, "I can accept you as you are, but can you?" In other instances words of Scripture may come unbidden to mind and be discerned as God's answer to the person's self-revelation. People who have let the word of God speak to them and have reacted honestly to it will know from experience the kind of dialogue that can ensue.

The dialogue takes place, then, between the living word and the responsive hearer of the word. It is not, even when Scripture forms its basis, a study session, though prior study can add to its richness. Study can become a substitute for dialogue and so thwart the dialogic purpose of the word.

The stereotype of the pale, emaciated ascetic who has developed total control of all his reactions and reponses does not fit our description of the responsive hearer of the word. That controlled a person would be a poor candidate for the kind of spiritual direction that makes relationship a central focus. The best candidates are those who have lived life and not been afraid of its joys and pains. They have been able to develop close relationships with other people. And they have strong desires for something more in their relationship with God. These desires may come from a sense of emptiness in spite of success in work or in raising a family, a sense of something lacking that often seems to come to people after thirty-five. They may come because of the cultural and social and religious malaise we alluded to in Chapter 2. Life crises may disturb the equilibrium of some and force them to ask about the quality of their lives with God. The death of a parent or spouse or close friend, for example, or the onset of a severe illness or a change of job or of community—such crises can occasion a new look at one's relationship with God and lead to a desire for something more.

In our experience the people who are most comfortable with and desirous of the kind of relationship to God and the kind of spiritual direction we are describing are generally active, vibrant, earthy, intelligent Christians, a far cry from the usual stereotype of the "spiritual" person. They are as real as rain, fog, and sunshine. They want to let God be himself to them. They have strong desires for intimacy and they make good friends and lovers. They are responsive people and so can be responsive to the word.

But they are also human and so all their responses do not emerge at once. They need to grow in relationship to God and in the ability to deepen their dialogue with him. As they continue to respond to the word, reactions not at first apparent progressively enter the dialogue. A man may initially react with approval to the word he hears, for instance, and then, after hours of enjoyment of the dialogue, find himself expressing anger to God. It may even take him some time to recognize that it is anger that he is expressing. Or a woman's initial reaction to the word may be anger, but in a short time her anger may give way to an appreciation that God can accept her as angry, and then to an acceptance of his concern.

In this continuing dialogue a person's deepest reactions to the action of God may come into explicit engagement only very slowly. They may become engaged, too, only with considerable difficulty. Some of our reactions take on protective coloration, for example. A man who is angry at God will often not listen and respond to him in prayer. Consequently, he may not pray at all. Rarely, though, will he say to himself that he is not praying because he is angry at God. Instead, he may tell himself that he does not pray because he has no time. He may even ask a spiritual director to help him work out a schedule that will allow him time for prayer, and spend months vainly trying to locate a place in his schedule for regular prayer. These efforts at scheduling will not result in frequent prayer, however, because they will not help him address the reason for his lack of prayer. He is too angry to listen to God, but believes that he is too undisciplined or too busy to pray.

Sometimes, therefore, the reasons we give ourselves for not praying are not the real reasons. Often enough the real reasons will be attitudes in ourselves that we find hard to accept. Who wants to know, for instance, that he is angry at God, dubious about his marriage, or deeply afraid of life? Yet, if personal prayer is to be frequent and tolerable, we will have to let ourselves increasingly communicate our real attitudes to God. "Transparent" is an apt description of the attitude of openness that develops as we let the Word speak to us and let our response to him represent ourselves and our attitudes more fully.

People are often surprised to find that one exposure of a strong feeling like anger in prayer does not eliminate this feeling as a factor in their relationship with God, and so does not eliminate the necessity for repeated expression of it. "I've already said it all!" is a common expression of their frustration. The feeling keeps recurring, however, and thus may need to be expressed again and again in the prayer. The repeated appearance of an unwanted feeling when we pray does not imply that God did not understand us the first time we expressed it or that we have failed to express ourselves adequately. It means rather that the development of transparency in our relationship with him requires repeated expressions of a particular feeling. The feeling continues and may reappear each time we pray, just as a feeling we may have toward a close friend may reappear each time we talk with the friend. In a friendship between two human beings the recurrence of anger or shyness does not mean that the friendship is failing. So too, the recurrence, even the frequent recurrence, of unwanted feelings toward God or the universe he has made does not mean that the relationship with him is in danger of collapse. What endangers a friendship is not anger or shyness or any other unwanted feeling, but an unwillingness on the part of one person or the other to share his feelings and the buildup of alienation that can result. The frequency with which people describe an emotional alienation from God in prayer indicates that such a buildup has occurred more often than is commonly realized.

Emotional alienation, however, does not imply an offense against God or moral failure in any sense to which we are accustomed. It may, however, imply a failure to grow in relationship. One of the ways in which failure to grow in relationship is manifested makes the lack of growth dramatically obvious. Some people pray as they did when they were children. They think and act as adults and have the responsibilities of adults, but when they pray, they use the same tone and speak within the same framework of expectations they used when they were ten years old. In addressing God, for example, a woman who has just lost her only child may be able to use no tone but one of thanks or petition. She may not be able to express in prayer her sense of loss and outrage. The language of prayer she is accustomed to cannot support such feelings because ten year-olds cannot afford to be angry at someone as great and awesome as God. There may also be another reason: she may find it hard to express deep feelings of sorrow or anger to anyone, even to admit them to herself.

Transparency grows, then, as we become more aware that, in our experience, God is trustworthy, and as we become better able to express our own deeper attitudes to him. This expression of attitude requires further explanation. It is not a terse statement like: "I am grateful," for instance. It is rather a lengthy, patient attempt to say one's feeling, mood, or attitude to the Lord. It is done in much the same way a person expresses his inner self in its state of the moment to a close friend who, he knows, will not desert him or become alienated from him no matter what he says. A man might say, for example, that God's care for him moves him almost to tears, that he feels he cannot repay it, and that he feels guilty because he cannot. He will try to communicate the mood or the feelings themselves and do so as directly as possible. He may cry. If he is a voluble person who expresses deep gratitude most directly by unaccustomed silence, he may be quiet for ten or fifteen minutes. If he expresses gratitude best with bodily gestures, he may remain for five minutes in a profound bow. Anger or fear can also be expressed directly—with expletives, gestures, expostulation, an eloquent recounting of the incident or situation that has provoked the feeling, or with other means of direct expression of emotion.

The more experience we have of prayer, the more likely we are to let more than thought enter our prayer. We will find ourselves spontaneously seeking ways of expressing ourselves more fully. An attempt to be receptive to God or to communicate with him that does not involve voice, gesture, or other activity often seems impoverished and superficial, and may be experienced as somehow unreal. Ascetical practices such as fasting may at times arise from this need to be more fully expressive. They allow the body to express attitude, and so enable the person to enter more fully into communication with God. Thus, inviting God to communicate with us in prayer and trying to respond to him in prayer tend to involve all of ourselves. Feeling, mood, thought, desire, hope, will, bodily gestures and attitudes, activity and direction of life tend to be affected. The prayer deepens, and as it does, it gradually draws into its dynamic more and more of our powers and resources. Its scope broadens too. Gradually it draws within its dynamic more and more dimensions of our lives. Our social and economic attitudes, our interpersonal relationships, our choice of friends, our choice of work, all begin to be affected by the relationship between ourselves and God as that relationship is expressed in personal prayer.

Prayer does not take place in isolation from the rest of a person's interests. Its scope and texture are both affected by them. A person living in close and friendly contact with the people of a Sioux reservation will find his own prayer affected by both the contemplative attitudes of his Sioux associates and by the cultural impasse in which they live. The administrator of a school in which most of the students are poor will discover that her prayer is affected by her responsibilities and, if she is a compassionate woman, by the social situation of her students. The powerlessness that Jesus chooses for himself and his sympathy with the poor will have a different meaning and a different affective impact on her than it will have on a Harvard professor, for example. Her other interests are in turn affected by what happens to her in communicative prayer. She will tend to become more compassionate, more patient with other people's feelings, more tolerant of her own. She is likely to have a broader vision, greater openness to change in society and in her environment, for instance.

There are undoubtedly people whom prayer isolates from the currents of life around them and makes impervious to social need. Most of us have heard of pious churchgoers who have presided over oppressive governments. We wish we could say that such incongruities are rare, but we have no evidence that they are. The word "prayer" is not always used to designate communicative prayer or even attempts at communicative prayer. It often refers to rote recitation of set prayers, passive attendance at a liturgy, the performance of a duty. In such prayer what is communicated to God may be no more than a desire to be on his good side. In contrast, the kind of truly communicative prayer we have been describing changes people and, if it continues, ultimately brings them to examine the whole of their lives.

At the same time, we must remember that we come to prayer, even communicative prayer, as people with a history, a social and cultural milieu, a specific religious upbringing and catechesis. We do not shed our past as a snake sheds its old skin. Spiritual directors need to know where their directees come from. The woman who still prays like a ten-year-old will not easily come to the point where she can tell God how outraged she is at the loss of her only child. She needs help to develop her relationship with God, not facile suggestions to "let it all hang out." Spiritual directors need to recognize the influence that years of training in good manners have on the prayer of many of their directees. A slow and patient pedagogy is often called for, a pedagogy that might include references to psalms (like Psalm 6 where anger and impatience at God are expressed), to biblical descriptions of importunate requests (such as the story of blind Bartimaeus in Mark 10), to some helpful books on prayer, as well as painstaking, compassionate, and considerate help so that people become aware of unwanted feelings toward God and his world and are able to speak the truth they discover to him. Moreover, spiritual directors are not a person's only source of religious thought. The woman who lost her son, for example, may be hearing in sermons on Sunday that it is sinful to question God's actions or to be angry at him. It is not enough to dismiss such an influence as hopelessly benighted. The woman needs sympathetic help to thread her way through the confusion created by her own conflicted feelings and the conflicting "help" she is receiving; she needs help, in other words, to put herself with all her confusion and conflicted feelings before the Lord.

Finally, we need to remind ourselves that spiritual direction is only one of many ministries in the Church. Spiritual directors will learn much in their work about God and about people that will be helpful in their other Christian ministries. The more ministering people know about the ways of God with individuals, the better they will be able to teach, preach, visit the sick, prepare liturgical music, and do other ministries so that these ministries attain their ultimate purpose—to help people meet the living God. But spiritual directors have as their central task the facilitation of the relationship between directees and God. They offer direct help with that relationship. Teaching, preaching, and moral guidance are not the proper task of spiritual directors. Their task is to help people experience God's action and respond to him. Fostering discovery rather than teaching doctrine is their purpose.

We have found it necessary to stress this point because of the almost universal and deeply entrenched tendency of ministering people to want to inculcate truth, to teach, to instruct. This tendency rears its head so quickly that beginning spiritual directors often do not listen well to the experience of their directees and as a result do not hear all the nuances of their experience of and reasoning about God. Once they have learned that their proper task is to facilitate discovery, however, they become able appropriately to introduce theological clarifications and reflections.

It is startling, when one reflects on the matter, that help directly aimed at the personal worship of God in spirit and in truth should ever have been regarded as only one of many pastoral concerns, and a somewhat esoteric concern at that. It seems rather that it should be the core from which all the Church's other pastoral care radiates. For spiritual direction, if it performs its proper task, must help people to recognize and focus their lives as response to God's loving, creative, and saving action. Unless they have had some experience of such recognition and focussing, Christians will treat all descriptions of interior attitudes as objective data, as meaningful—and as meaningless—as an almanac list of historical events. Systematic and moral theology, spirituality and liturgical studies will give them objective knowledge, but will have little to do with the crucial wants and nonnegotiable values of their lives. As objects of study these may fascinate, but as objects of study they also exist outside the growth, risk, shakiness, joy, and depression Christians experience, and so they leave their hearts untouched.

A spiritual direction that stems from the heart of the Christian tradition has no axes to grind, no pet theories on which its efficacy depends. It is primarily concerned with helping individuals freely to place themselves before God who will communicate himself to them and make them more free. The focus of the direction is on the Lord and the way he seems to relate to each person, never on ideas.

Our experience affirms that it is this kind of direction that mature, experienced, active Christians want. They look on spiritual jargon—terms like consolation, desolation, "the two standards"—with suspicion. They are likely to be disturbed by a director's bias against either personal responsibility or authority. They are wary of fanaticism, whether of the right or the left, and they eschew sentimentalism. There are few, if any, visions. There is, however, a strong desire to know and encounter God as the central Christian spiritual tradition has known and encountered him.

In a time and place where attitudes toward the churches and the pastoral care they provide are often in flux, people who are growing with the help of this kind of direction frequently sense an increasing desire to know Christian teaching about God and the Christian life. They ask only that it be the kind of teaching they can relate to their experience. They also become increasingly amenable to other forms of pastoral care, not because they are exhorted to accept them, or even because these other forms have been suggested to them. Their increasing aliveness simply makes them more interested. By the same token, deadness and venality in the Church's ministry may make them angry—and likely to do something about their anger. Those who are being freed by the Lord are not always comfortable companions. As Jesus was not always a comfortable companion.

4

Fostering the Contemplative Attitude

What does a spiritual director do?

Everyone who engages in spiritual direction will answer this question differently. The way we list and formulate the tasks of the director will depend on the way we envision the needs of the spiritual life and the estimate we make of our own capabilities. In any carefully drawn list some place will be given to (1) empathetic listening, (2) paying attention, (3) affirming, (4) assisting in clarification, (4) raising questions when the directee wants them, and (5) helping the directee to recognize the affective attitudes that influence his attitude to God. All of these activities—and others—are indispensable to the work of direction. We could get lost in the list. More important, we could become so concerned with performing all these tasks well that we might lose sight of the reason people come for direction. Faced with this possibility one may have to ask oneself: What are the most fundamental tasks of the director?

Let us propose that there are two, and that they issue from this insight: the contemplative core of prayer and of all Christian life is conscious relationship with God. The tasks are:

First, helping the directee pay attention to God as he reveals himself;

Second, helping the directee recognize his reactions and decide on his responses to this God.

We will discuss these tasks separately. This separation is not intended to indicate that in practice they occur separately, and that the first must be completed before the second is begun. Often God reveals himself and the person reacts and responds almost simultaneously, and the director frequently, even usually, will perform both tasks in the same conversation. However, for the sake of clarity and some thoroughness in approaching both tasks, we will discuss them separately.

Relationships develop only when the persons involved pay attention to one another. We make an assumption based on Christian tradition that God is taking his part in the relationship, is paying attention to the directee, is looking at and listening to him or her. The directee, however, if the relationship is to develop, must also pay attention to the Lord. This is not a complex matter, but it is not necessarily easy either. There is, first of all, the difficulty we human beings have in paying attention to anyone else. Then there is the difficulty of paying attention to the invisible, mysterious, and all-powerful God.

The people who come for spiritual direction are usually not neophytes in faith or in prayer. They have been believers and praying people for some time, but now they are looking for something more. But often the prayer to which they have been accustomed is not contemplative. Prayer, for many, has meant the use of set prayers like the "Lord's Prayer," the Book of Common Prayer, the psalms, the Rosary, petitionary prayer, meditation from a book of meditations, or the pondering of problems or questions. Many people have, however, been surprised by God through these practices. One seventy-five-year-old woman said that sometimes she "goes deep" while saying her set prayers and then she knows she is really talking to God and he is listening. The depth of the kind of prayer people are accustomed to should not, therefore, be underestimated. But it is not usually contemplative and is not as conducive to a conscious growth in relationship as is contemplation. Contemplation of its nature gives more room for the Lord to take on a reality of his own.

What is contemplation? We are not here using the word in its mystical meaning. We are using it in a sense that is closer to the meaning Ignatius of Loyola gave it when he proposed (in his *Spiritual Exercises*) that a person look at Jesus as he appears in gospel events and let himself become absorbed in what he is like, what he cares about, and what he is doing. Contemplation in this sense begins when a person stops being totally preoccupied with his own concerns and lets another person, event, or object take his attention. When it is a person who is being contemplated, he lets that person, with his personality, concerns, and activity take his attention. He lets himself be absorbed, for a moment at least, and at some level, in the other person. Contemplative prayer, as we use the term here, means paying attention to and becoming at least slightly absorbed in the person of Jesus, in God, or in biblical persons or outstanding Christians. A contemplative attitude can develop from such prayer and, if it does, it allows one to find some ease and spontaneity in paying attention to the Lord as he reveals himself in Scripture, creation, one's own life, and the life of the world, rather than seeing him simply as a background figure for one's own concerns.

There are two difficulties, however, that must be overcome if a person is to have some facility in this kind of contemplation. The first is caused by the prior categories that often make it next to impossible to see and hear any "other" in his or her or its own right. We do not see the individual because we have already relegated what we see to a class: "another eucalyptus tree," "another sunset," "a German." The second has to do with our tendency to look inward rather than outward, to be absorbed in our own concerns rather than in another person's. We have notions of prayer that preclude or attenuate looking and listening. We think of prayer as looking inward. When we hear the words "Let us pray," we automatically bow our heads and close our eyes. Often too, prayer is seen basically as petition, as thinking something through, or as getting insights. And all these activities, while good in themselves, tend to preclude looking and listening. Spiritual directors must often work patiently and creatively if directees are to experience contemplation and see themselves as contemplative people.

If you have ever been so absorbed in watching a game, reading a book, or listening to music that you have been surprised at how much time has passed, by how cold or hot you are, by the anger of a friend who has been asking a question for a few minutes, then you know the power of paying attention to something, and you have a personal example of the contemplative attitude. Parents have been so concerned about their children in fires and accidents that they become aware of their own injuries only after the emergency has ended. Soldiers in battle have become aware of wounds only after the fighting has stopped.

Thus, one effect of paying attention to something outside ourselves is that it can make us forget ourselves and our surroundings. Contemplation leads to, or rather is an experience of, transcendence—that is, of forgetfulness of self and of everyone and everything else except the contemplated object.

Conversely, self-absorption makes the contemplation of anything or anyone else very difficult, if not impossible. Thus, a starving man will not enjoy a sunset. A student preparing in great anxiety for an examination may not notice a conversation taking place beside him.

Spiritual directors sometimes have to work long and patiently with people to help them reach the point of being able to forget themselves. Self-absorption can even mask itself unconsciously as virtue. For instance, a man who concentrates on his failings and sins may be considered and consider himself an honest, self-knowledgeable man; yet he may never change his behavior. When he reads Scripture, he hears the words of condemnation and applies them to himself; but he never hears the words of forgiveness and freedom and never sees the look of love that the Lord casts on the sinner. It becomes apparent that "humility" and "self-knowledge" are in his case synonyms for self-absorption.

The spiritual director will have to help such a person to

forget himself and his problems and to look at the Lord. The help may begin with assistance in looking at and listening to something other than himself—music, natural beauty, art, architecture, or anything else that will absorb him. Self-absorption is a concentration on weakness. The effort to help a person to look beyond himself is part of the appeal to strength that is the task of the spiritual director.[1]

Another aspect of contemplation deserves our attention. The reactions of absorption, joy, pain, sympathy, love, and gratitude that are associated with contemplation are not willed. They are elicited from us by what we see, hear, and comprehend. Although conditioned by our past experiences, they are basically spontaneous responses to people and things outside ourselves. Here we have an important element to consider in spiritual direction. The clearest example, perhaps, is the reaction of love when one looks at the beloved. It seems to be a gift, something that arises because of the other, not because of any decision of one's own to love or to fall in love. Directors help people to realize that they can look at and try to pay attention to what God has done, is doing, has said, is saying, but that they cannot will their reactions. At most, they can hope that they will react in a certain way. But if a woman, for example, does not react as she had hoped—if instead of joy she feels anger at the words "O Lord, thou has searched me and known me"[2]—she has nonetheless reacted, and she can choose to express her reaction to the Lord. She can choose, too, to ask the Lord to help her with her anger.

The person contemplating can have no control over the other. One cannot force a sunset to be brilliant. All one can do is to hope and to look. Contemplation leads to an attitude of reverence and wonder before the other. If the other is a person, then all we can do is ask him to reveal himself and wait for that to happen. This insight is the reason for the prayer for what one desires that Ignatius of Loyola puts at the beginning of each of the exercises of the *Spiritual Exercises*. At one point the retreatant is asked to pray that the Lord will reveal his sinfulness to him so that he may have shame and confusion. At another point the retreatant prays that the Lord make himself known to him so that he may love him and follow him.[3]

Here the relationship between contemplation and transcendence appears even more clearly. When we are dealing with another person, we are not in the same position as when we are dealing with an object. Saint-Exupéry's Little Prince on his asteroid only needs to move his chair a bit in order to see another sunset, but he is powerless to see the reality and uniqueness of his flower until she chooses to reveal herself to him.[4]

Spiritual directors encourage their directees to ask for what they want from the Lord. In the beginning their desires may be very broad: to experience God's presence, to know him better, for instance. Such requests should reflect their real desires, and part of the work of spiritual directors is to help directees to clarify and say what they really want. The directee, then, at the beginning of a period of contemplation, first asks for what he wants, then looks at or listens to whatever happens in the contemplation. In other words, he places himself in relationship with the other person by asking that he reveal himself and then pays attention to the One being revealed.

To pray for the Lord's self-revelation opens us to the mystery of the Other. Such openness runs counter to much of our usual personal activity. We try to control our perceptions; we are threatened by newness and strangeness. As a result, we often see only what we want to see or what our perceptual and cognitive structures let us see. To try to contemplate means to try to let the other be himself or herself or itself, to try to be open to surprise and newness, to try to let one's responses be elicited by the reality of the other. So, when we contemplate God, we try to let him be himself and not our projection of him, and to be real ourselves before him.

The actual experience of transcendence falls somewhere between total self-absorption and total absorption in the other. In any human experience there is bound to be a mixture of both self-consciousness and awareness of the outside world. Spiritual directors can help directees to realize that the contemplation of the Lord is no different from the contemplation of any other person in this regard; one can be in the intimate presence of a very dear friend and still be aware of the ache in one's feet, of wondering whether one put out the lights in the car, of the work still to be done for class tomorrow. "Distractions," in other words, occur even in the most intimate relationships and should be expected in prayer too.

Finally, in an intimate conversation, reflection on what is happening or on how well one is contemplating (especially with the idea of writing about it in one's journal or using it as an example for a chapter like this) is an instance of self-absorption and can disturb the communication. The director can help people avoid this disturbance by suggesting that they do their reflection after the period of prayer is over.

In the beginning phases of spiritual direction, directors usually have to help people to contemplate the Lord. What kind of help do directees need? They usually find that intensity and effort in looking at or listening to God are not very helpful; these usually end in self-absorption. They would benefit more from spending time at first in some activity they enjoy that has a contemplative aspect to it. This might be anything from bird-watching to admiring the architecture of a city, from listening to the surf to listening to Bach—any receptive experience that helps a person forget himself and become absorbed in something else. The person might consider this experience one that he shares with the Lord in much the same way that he might want to share it with a close friend. We also suggest that people ask the Lord to make his presence known, to reveal himself during this time. Then they look at or listen to what it is they enjoy. After each period of doing this we ask them to reflect on the experience: What happened? What did they experience? Did the Lord make himself known?

It is surprising to observe what happens when people begin to do something like this. At first they may object that such nonreligious activity cannot be prayer. Moreover, since prayer for them has often meant brooding, insights, and resolutions, they often need time and patience to become accustomed to this new way of prayer and to find out that the director really means what he says. Then, however, they begin to find such prayer times enjoyable and relaxing. They find themselves surprised by feelings of joy and gratitude and a sense that Someone is present who loves and cares for them. They often find that they can admit things to themselves that they were always afraid or ashamed to look at, and they begin to feel freed, healed.

These reflections bring us to the question: Are there any privileged places or privileged events to which we can go to put ourselves more explicitly in the Lord's way? The traditional answer has been that there are, and that they include the sacraments, especially the Eucharist, Church teaching, the Scriptures, and the other works of the Lord, especially nature. Nature and the Scriptures are the privileged places most often recommended by spiritual directors and so deserve particular attention.

Traditionally people have found peace and refreshment in the beauty of nature. The fact that most retreat houses, houses of prayer, and monasteries have been located in or near scenes of natural beauty testifies to the common belief that we find God more easily in such locales than we do in urban environments.[5] The Judeo-Christian tradition, moreover, has persistently spoken of God as revealing himself in the things he has made. Without intending to say that the countryside and the seashore are the only places where the Lord can be met (for he is present in the city, too, and there seem to be times when spectacular natural beauty is a distraction from prayer) the spiritual director often tries to help people to meet the Lord and listen to him by encouraging them to look first at natural beauty.

When they try to help people to contemplate God in nature, directors should suggest that they look and listen and not give them ideas to ponder—ideas, for example, about continuing creation and the indwelling of the Spirit. Most of us have been accustomed by reading, by courses in Church teaching, and perhaps by philosophy and theology classes to the truth that God is in all things, but few of us have ever looked long enough at a flower to let God reveal himself as the maker of that flower for me. Before I can see a tree as an embodiment of God's activity, I must first see it, touch it, and smell it as a tree. First of all, then, the director suggests that people look at and listen to what is around them.

The second suggestion for the contemplation of nature is that looking at natural beauty can in itself be a way of relating to the Lord. Words are not necessary. Just as I relate to an artist by taking an interest in what she has made, by taking time to look at it or listen to it, so too I can relate to God by contemplating what he has made. Creators like to have people show interest in what they have done. They enjoy our interest still more if we like what we see and smile or sigh or express delight in their presence. Such responses are elicited by what we contemplate, not willed by us, and they are communications to the artist. When the artist is God, the communications are called prayers of praise. They do not have to be couched in "prayer language." Indeed the prayer is often made before a word is formed. When a person has begun to react to natural beauty, then the spiritual director might point out that these responses are similar to the responses of the author of Psalm 104, responses which he expressed poetically. Not everyone is a poet, but almost everyone can be thrilled by a dazzling sunset or sunrise, or by the sun's light on fall leaves, and feel a deep sense of wonder.

People contemplating may not, however, be content with looking at the beauties of nature and admiring God's handiwork. They may also want God to reveal himself, to speak personally to them. They begin their period of contemplation by asking that he make himself known. Does he respond? How will they know? The question here is directly concerned with the ordinary ways in which God reveals himself, not with mystical experience—although such experience occurs more often than we sometimes realize.

A woman might be walking along a beach at night and see the moon touch with silver the crest of a wave. She delights in the sight and suddenly feels at peace and in the presence of Someone else who himself delights in such things. Unaccountably she may feel that she is still loved, even though she does drink or eat too much, get angry with her family too often, or has just lost a job, and she may feel free to face herself more honestly and with less self-pity. Or a young man might sense his insignificance under the stars, and yet feel that he is important in the whole scheme of things. Or a man quietly looking at a mountain peak wreathed in cloud might sense a call deep inside himself to change his way of life. In all these instances these people may be hearing or sensing the voice of the Lord revealing himself. When the experiences are keenly felt and exciting and challenging as well as comforting, the Lord may have begun to take on a new reality for them.

We can look at the contemplation of Scripture in a similar way. Scripture is not the Lord, but a privileged place to meet him. However, one must pay attention to Scripture in the same way that in the contemplation of nature one has to pay attention to trees or sunsets or mountains. One must have a contemplative attitude toward Scripture, let the Scriptures be themselves, listen to them, and ask that the Lord reveal himself while we are listening.

There is no reason why spiritual directors should have to argue about whether other religious texts might also be privileged places for meeting God. History and contemporary experience tell us that many other texts have been and are such privileged places. We are accepting as given, however, the fact that the Bible has primacy of place for Christians as the word of God.

It is good to listen to the Scriptures themselves, not our projections onto them. Spiritual directors, like everyone else, have been affected by modern scriptural scholarship. They may wonder how they can use Scripture to help their directees in prayer, for we moderns have many questions about what Jesus actually said or did. If the search for the historical Jesus has been such a problem for modern biblical scholars, can we still use the gospels to come to know him?

The first point to be made is an obvious one: It is not finally helpful for prayer or Christian living to base it on a delusion. Hence, it is important to see the gospels for what they are. They are not biographies of Jesus, but four different expressions of the faith of the early Church and what it remembered in faith about Jesus. Each gospel has its own point of view, its own theological focus, its own life situation. Contemplation of Mark's gospel, for example, means taking that author's work on its own terms and trying to listen to his work as he meant it to be heard.

Secondly, it should be said that one need not be a Scripture scholar to use the gospels for prayer. The Lord can still reveal himself to a person who believes that angels did sing "Glory to God in the highest" at Bethlehem provided that the person is willing to let the living Lord reveal himself. But the more one knows about a gospel, the better one can look at and listen to it and not to one's own cultural and personal projections onto it. Thus, Scripture study can be a help to contemplation. To be able to contemplate Mark's Jesus and know that it is Mark's Jesus one is contemplating and not necessarily Jesus in all his historical reality is a help to one's perspective. For one thing, one will not then be dismayed by every new discovery of biblical scholarship. More importantly still, one is emphatically aware that the Person one wants to meet is not the Jesus of the past, but the present living Lord whom we believe and experience in faith as continuous with Jesus of Nazareth.[6]

Now we are at the heart of the matter for spiritual direction. The purpose of contemplating the gospels is to come to know the living Lord Jesus. Once again the wisdom of Ignatius of Loyola as a director becomes apparent. Before every contemplation of events from the gospels, he has retreatants pray for what they desire: "an intimate knowledge of our Lord, who has become man for me that I may love Him more and follow Him more closely."[7] Then they listen to the gospel text and treat it for what it is: literature intended to teach people how to let it inspire their imaginations and enkindle their faith as it was written to do. But the desire is not to know the Scripture text better. Rather it is to know Jesus better.

Often in spiritual direction a conversation like the following will occur: (Mary is the directee, John the director.)

Mary: I was really struck by Jesus in the cleansing-of-the-temple scene.
John: How did he seem to you?
Mary: He seemed very angry.
John: Angry?
Mary: Yes, He seemed so thoroughly involved in what God deserved and in the contrast between that and what those people were actually doing.
John: He seemed very involved with it. That seemed important for you. Could you say more about it?
Mary: About the way it seemed to me?
John: Yes, about what he was like.

The director in this exchange is helping the directee to concentrate on what Jesus seemed like in the prayer. A number of his comments seem banal. Their purpose is to do no more than help the directee to keep looking at her own impression of Jesus. He does not try, at this point at least, to encourage the directee to look at implications of Jesus' action for her own life. He does not yet ask the directee how she felt about her impression of Jesus. He simply helps her to stay focussed on Jesus and on what he is doing.

Often when a director has had this experience of helping the directee to focus on Jesus and what he is like, he finds that the directee has seen more than she realizes and that

Jesus' actions have a significance for her that she has not yet recognized. Let us continue with the exchange.

Mary: Well, he was angry, as I said. He was really involved with the merchants doing business in the temple.

John: Why don't you take a minute now and look back on the way that scene seemed to you? You seem to have been engaged by it.

Mary: (Pause.) He really felt a lot about God. He seemed to feel that God was being insulted and that bothered him.

John: It bothered him?

Mary: Got under his skin. You know, it really seemed to affect him the way an insult given to somebody in your family who is dear to you might affect you. (Pause.) That's what it seemed like.

John: And that seemed to be a moving thing for you?

Mary: It was. I've experienced things like that, harsh things, for example, said about people who meant a lot to me, so I could appreciate how he felt. It made me feel somehow more familiar with him.

John's willingness to help Mary to look at the impression she has received in her prayer has in this second part of the dialogue resulted in her expressing and apparently seeing more clearly something that seems important to her. If the director had not offered her an opportunity to continue looking, she would not have spoken of this development and perhaps would not have seen it. As a result of seeing it, she has begun to speak spontaneously of her feeling reaction to Jesus. The contemplative dialogue can now continue at this depth.

Experienced directors will recognize that helping people to look more persistently at the Lord in prayer and to express what they have seen is not always as easy as it appears here. Directors will often feel that asking the question, "When you prayed, what was the Lord like?" is a futile enterprise because the answer so often is "I don't know." Many people do not seem to think in those terms when they pray. Yet if the person coming for direction wants to be closer to the Lord, it is important to help him keep looking at the way the Lord seemed to him. We do not come closer to anyone by not knowing what the person is like. The fact seems to be that people who pray continue to pray because they do have impressions that the Lord is attractive and inviting. It is, however, very difficult for them to express this. Is the effort worthwhile?

The way directors answer this question has a great deal of effect on the kind of direction they give. Persistent returning to looking at what the Lord is like when she prays can gradually develop Mary's ability to see her prayer as dialogic. Her perception of the Lord as he appears in the prayer will gradually become keener. As a result, she will react more frequently and more fully to him. The prayer thus comes to take on a life of its own.

It is not that questions like, "What does this mean for your life?" cannot be asked when we are talking about prayer. The issue is, rather, whether the director will help Mary see what the Lord is like to her in the prayer before he begins to help her look at implications. In other words, he tries to help her engage with the contemplative substance of her prayer and does not sacrifice that effort to attempts to get at meaning.

Some directors may feel that the people they direct cannot talk about religious experience, or that religious experience is not an important factor in their prayer. Perhaps they have not been persistent about pursuing the question, "What is the Lord like?" As a result, the people they talk with have not really looked at what he is like for them. It may be that it is not a matter of their being led in another direction by the Lord but a matter of the director not helping them recognize what can happen if they pay attention to him.

If directors do help directees to pay attention to the Lord, they find that the simple act of looking at the Lord in a scriptural event, or in some other event or situation, is in itself productive prayer. This contemplation produces, all by itself, sprouts of love, affection, and desire; and these in turn lead the person to look more closely at the Lord. The looking more closely can gradually bring about a new trust in him or companionship with him. The search for meaning, while valid in itself, can in the context of contemplation be a distraction from this process. The person has to judge which of the two is more likely to result in the relationship he wants.

The experience of people who pray seems to show us that the contemplation we have described has led them to deeper choices that are more involved with the wellsprings of their lives than the choices they make outside the ambience of this contemplation. This is another reason why "staying with the directee" can be one of the most valuable services the director renders. It is not a service that builds up the director's sense of self-importance, however. He does nothing but act as the servant of the contemplation that takes place in a directee's prayer. And everything he does in this staying with the contemplation is aimed at focussing on the way the directee is seeing the Lord and on avoiding letting himself and the directee get distracted from it.

A final word remains to be said about our list of privileged places. Those mentioned are still found to be privileged places by many people. At the same time, different people may prefer some places to others. It may also be that new privileged places may come to the fore. In particular, the modern shift from contact with nature to more contact with man-made works may have made these works a newly privileged place. Joseph Sudbrack, the German spiritual theologian, makes this point and also urges spiritual directors to keep an open eye for the many and often surprising human situations that can serve as beginning points for prayer.[8] Morton Kelsey makes a strong case for attention to dreams, pointing out that many of the Church Fathers used dreams in their spiritual direction.[9] Spiritual directors need to be aware of the broad range of possibly privileged places in order to help their directees find the best place for them to stand as they wait for the Lord to reveal himself.

When the Lord readily becomes real for a person like Mary and she readily lets herself be completely real with the Lord, prayer changes and, on the whole, stays changed. God ceases to be distant and abstract. He is closer in life, present in prayer, and has values and a will of his own. He is not a function of morality, but accepts, loves, and often challenges the imperfect person. He can be spoken to, and through the communication that takes place in prayer and life he moves to transform the person and bring her toward the maturity of Christ. Thus, when Mary looks at the Lord through the images of Scripture, for example, she sees a Lord who is not controlled by her own preferences and needs, a Lord who often walks on unknown roads and says unexpected things. The person looked at, in other words, begins obviously to take on a life of his own, even though his autonomy will usually still be limited by the directee's subconscious conceptions. When the Lord begins, then, to be seen more clearly with this life of his own in the directee's prayer, the director will usually recognize that his own contribution will depend first of all on his ability not to interfere with the dialogue that is going on, secondly on his ability to facilitate that dialogue—that is, to encourage a person like Mary to listen and respond from her heart.

The primacy of this task of noninterfering facilitation is easy enough to understand when the contemplative attitude is sufficiently developed to be recognized. However, the implications of this primacy are not confined to the time when a contemplative attitude has been developed. They should be clear to directors throughout the process of direction. Even when directees experience only their own anger, fear, or guilt in prayer and do not dream of a prayer in which the Lord could begin to take on a life of his own, directors must remember what their primary task is and help directees to move toward the contemplation that will be. In their direction then, they use no approach that will hamper the development of contemplation, and they introduce into the direction no elements that, however helpful they might seem at the time, will distort or confuse the contemplative attitude when it does clearly appear.[10]

Thus for practical purposes, spiritual direction can be divided into two major phases, or kinds. The dividing line between the two is the experience, however dim, of the Lord's reality. It should be obvious that we are not speaking of mystical prayer. The contemplative experience will take different forms in different persons, and different forms in the same person at different times, yet in all forms there is an experience of the Lord's reality. He may become awesome and daunting, or loving and inviting, or enigmatic and disconcerting. He will often be seen as healing, making whole. Often, too, he will be present but waiting for the person to take the step that must be taken if he is to be free. When a person has been sufficiently freed from anxieties, angers, and other fixations to be able to care about the Lord's love for his people, he will be seen as inviting him to share in his mission, to care for his people as he cares, to go the journey that he goes, sharing both its light and its darkness.

Through all these ways in which the Lord shows himself, the common element is his reality. He is not an idea to be thought about, a set of values to be considered, an image to be handled by the imagination. The person praying has the sense that he is not controlling the way the Lord seems to him. Someone else is setting the direction of the relationship, deciding its events. The praying person does not look for helpful thoughts, work up feelings, or concoct images. He simply looks at the Lord as he appears in Scripture or in experience, puts himself before him as he is, and lets happen what will happen.

There is nothing fixed or unchangeable about contemplation or about the attitude toward life, the Lord, his people, and oneself that gradually develops from the experience of contemplative prayer. The person in whom this attitude is developing may still sometimes balk at the need to expose a disagreeable attitude to the Lord and instead may withdraw into thinking about it or worrying about it; but if he is well into the development of the contemplative attitude, he will know when he is withdrawing from dialogue or will recognize it with relative ease.

The person may well not find prayer easy either. "Contemplative" often suggests repose to us, but contemplative prayer can be a wrestling match, too, and when in such bouts a person backs away from encounter, he may find that the Lord seems vague and distant. The important thing is that he knows from experience that dialogue is available to him should he be willing to enter it.

It is to be repeated here that the contemplative experience we are talking about is neither ethereal nor "extraordinary." It is as earthy as muddy boots, and as much involved with life. Its very earthiness and involvement with everyday life are indications of its authenticity. The anticontemplative bias is so strong in America, however, that when contemplation is described, many readers inevitably think: "Real life is too complex and difficult for a lot of people, so he's encouraging them to withdraw into the world of the mind, where reality is simpler and easier to control." This is precisely not true of contemplation as we are describing it. The person with an active vocation becomes more wholly, deeply, and passionately involved in the Lord's concern for his people and in their needs. The only element likely to be lost to the active life through contemplation is egocentricity.

The contemplative experience constitutes a dividing line in spiritual direction not because direction becomes easier once contemplation has begun, but because it becomes different. It may also become more demanding. When a person like Mary stops trying to make reality what she would like it to be and lets herself encounter reality as it chooses to be, the Spirit of the Lord is not the only spirit that can act in that new, freer atmosphere, and the director will be called on to help her develop ways of telling the difference between the benign and the destructive influences that affect her. She has now become less fixed in her egocentricity and less bogged down by it. But her desire to have life play the servant to her does not cease to lay claim on her. It becomes more volatile and more subtle, and consistently appears as an angel of light.

If the director has from the beginning of the direction seen his task as that of facilitating contemplation, his task now will probably not be excessively complicated by problems of dependence and confusion of goals. These problems will have been dealt with earlier, when it first became clear to the directee that the director's primary role was facilitative rather than instructional. "Why don't you take more initiative?" "Why don't you tell me what to do?" "Why don't you give me a structure to work with?" "Why don't you say more?" These are questions the director may have heard in the early meetings. Such questions, whether spoken or not, would have given the director opportunities to point out that responsibility for the directee's dialogue with the Lord lies with the Lord and the directee, not with the director. If the director took these opportunities then and waited for the directee to make some attempt to pay attention to the word and to ask the Lord to act, the direction is not likely to get bogged down, at this new point, in uncertainty about what is coming from the Lord and what is coming from the director, or in difficulties in distinguishing between what the directee really experiences and what she merely thinks she should experience. If, however, the director early in the process of direction explicitly, implicitly, even subliminally told the directee that he expected her to be a certain kind of person with a certain kind of relationship with God, and this expectation was not confronted and interred, then the experience of the directee during the contemplative phase is likely to be needlessly confusing at best, and at worst deeply misleading. If such confusion begins, the director may have no recourse except to try to form a new relationship with the directee or to refer her to another director.

5

Helping a Person Notice and Share with the Lord Key Interior Facts

Growth in a relationship requires that I pay attention to the other person. It also requires that I pay attention to what happens inside me when I am in the presence of the other and that I share my reactions with him. What does contemplation of the Lord do to me? I am only free to respond or not to respond to him when I am aware of the reactions I experience when I begin to pay attention to him. Noticing these reactions is fundamental to growth in the spiritual life, and helping a person notice and communicate them is one of the most fundamental tasks of spiritual direction.

We will limit the discussion at this point to the early stages of spiritual direction, to the time when the directee is often developing a rudimentary recognition of his spiritual identity. We do so not because attention to inner happenings is unimportant in later stages, but because that attention is easier to discuss as a separate operation in the early stages and because it usually has to be explicitly developed at that time. Resistance to noticing, for instance, appears more distinctly in these early stages and so lends itself more readily to description and discussion. It is in the early stages, too, that director and directee decide by the approach they take to one another whether the process of direction is to be basically instructional, chatty, or evocative. The choice of approaches is, therefore, of particular importance at this time, for it will determine the kind of relationship that will develop and the way in which direction can help.

It is from the directee's hopes and attitudes that the processes of direction and of spiritual growth develop. What is it like, then, to be beginning direction? An image may help here. The person beginning direction is like a traveler well started on a journey. He is far enough from his starting point to have recovered from the anxiety of preparation and the flurry of departure, but he is still far enough from his destination to be able to think of something other than arrival. He has begun to reflect on the journey itself, on what is happening to him on the road. He has begun to feel that these happenings have their own importance, and that ignoring them may somehow be missing the point of the journey and leaving him ill-prepared for his destination.

The person beginning spiritual direction is in much the same position as this traveler. His life and prayer do not begin with direction. It is, indeed, because his life included reflection and had a faith-dimension that he decided on direction. It has been a decision, not to begin life, but to live it more fully. When the first interviews with the director take place, he has, though he may not realize it, a great deal to say, and it is important that he at least make a start at saying it. For the direction must begin with the way the Lord is encountering him, not with some plan in the mind of the director. So he describes where he has been in life, what he has been looking for, what and whom he cares about, how he feels about his life, and where he wants to go. He describes, too, what has prompted him to look for direction. Through describing this body of experience he becomes more aware of it. Through the description the director also begins to be aware of this experience, and a common ground that will be the basis for direction begins to develop between them. If he can then submit the experience to God in prayer, ask for some awareness of his action in it, and discuss this experience of prayer with the director, the process of direction has been well begun.

However, this awareness and provision of a common ground are not always easily accomplished. Other factors are also important at the beginning of direction, for one thing. The development of the "just two people talking" atmosphere, in particular, is indispensable. If directors approach the directee's experience as research interviewers or policemen might, they will endanger the development of this atmosphere. Interviews with researchers and policemen do not create an atmosphere of "just two people talking." This atmosphere will have to develop at the same time as the growth of awareness and the common ground.

Then, too, most people are inarticulate when they try for the first time to describe their deeper feelings and attitudes. They can be even less articulate when they try to describe their relationship with God. "When you are looking at him in prayer, how did he seem?" is always, at first, a daunting question. People who can describe any other relationship in their lives in concrete, subjective terms go wide-eyed with consternation at this question. Often they fall back on purely objective descriptions such as "He is good, the Creator, holy," or, if they have some theological sophistication, "He is the uncaused cause, the ground of being." This inarticulateness constitutes a barrier that erodes slowly and cannot be breached by force. For to begin to talk about this aspect of their lives requires the equivalent of a new language, the ability to articulate inner experience.

This development of the ability to notice and to express what he notices can begin, then, with the person's first description of his life-experience and his reasons for deciding to engage in spiritual direction. The development continues in the first discussions of what is happening in his current prayer. At first he may say about the prayer of the previous week or two: "It was good. It was wonderful to get some time alone. The office was very busy." Or: "I didn't get much out of it.

The passages were interesting, but it was hard to keep my mind on them. Do you have any others?" To describe the experience of prayer, he needs the director's help in developing the new language. The director will have to say: "Let's talk a bit more about what happened. Which of those passages had most to say to you? What struck you about it? How did that make you feel?" Although a directee may occasionally ask: "What do you mean by 'feel'?" questions like these will usually help a person look more perceptively at his experience and encourage him to try to express what he sees there. At the start he may find his attention wavering and his expression halting, but the beginnings of fluency usually appear rather quickly when encouragement is given. As he becomes convinced that his experience is worth talking about, he notices it more readily, and soon becomes less diffident and more articulate in describing it.

As life affects us, God affects us, and as we react to life we react to him. The reaction may be generally positive: appreciation, enjoyment, a happy wonder, a cheerful willingness to accept vicissitudes and changing circumstances. Or it may be negative: We may resent, fear, or dislike what life is saying and doing to us. Or we may be happy about some things in our lives and irked, depressed, or hurt by others. Some of these reactions run much deeper than the person's conscious thought and motivate him more vitally. Any dialogue with the Lord that involves more than the surface of the person's life must take these deeper reactions into account, for they will influence prayer whether he wants them to or not.

The directee will have to notice these reactions to life, then, and bring them into prayer, if prayer is to become a personal enterprise rather than a mental exercise. The director can help him notice by pointing to the feelings that arise in a prayer that attempts to be dialogue with the Lord, and, when it promises to be helpful, discussing them. But he helps especially by pointing to the directee's feelings about his life that are becoming evident in their discussions and suggesting that he express them to the Lord.

It is when prayer first goes dry that noticing becomes most difficult—and most necessary. Because his efforts do not bring the comforting or dramatic results he expects, the person will probably describe the prayer by saying: "Nothing happened." He may be astonished the first time he spends an hour describing and discussing the "nothing." But that hour will prove crucially important for his understanding of prayer. Often, it is only in such discussions of seemingly barren prayer that directee and director can get at the concrete facts that express who the Lord is to the person and how the person is reacting to him. For when prayer runs dry at this stage of direction, it is usually because the level of dialogue on which prayer has been taking place has broken down, and the person is being invited to another level. The new level is always less general, less abstract, more deeply personal. As generalities and abstractions disappear, the bone structure of the person's relationship with God begins to appear. The director assists now by asking questions like: "What did the Scripture passage mean to you? How did it make you feel? Good or bad, happy, sad, apathetic, hopeful, discouraged? What did you say to him?" In this way he can help the directee notice the impressions of God and his own reactions to him that appeared in the prayer.

The director must keep his basic purpose in mind at this point. He is not looking for information, but encouraging the directee to notice inner facts. The conversation will consequently move more slowly and cover less ground than discussions usually do. The focus is on what happened, not on why it happened. So the director will often, without questioning or commenting, simply underscore emotional facts as they are presented: "I was frustrated." "You felt pretty frustrated." He will make comments that say nothing to the directee but "Do you notice how you felt about it?" To the directee's "I was wiped out for the rest of the day," he may reply: "You were pretty depressed." This underscoring, banal though it often sounds, gradually enables the directee to become more aware of emotional facts, and he shows this

increased awareness by describing those facts more spontaneously and extensively.

There are, however, occasions when simple repetition and
a minimum of interpretation will not be enough. When deep
fear, anger, sadness, or guilt are uncovered by dryness, they
will often have to be discussed at some length before the
person can accept them sufficiently to begin to recognize them
for himself and express them to the Lord.

The director's contribution to these conversations can be
summed up in two key questions: "Do you listen to the Lord
when you pray?" and "Are you telling him how listening to
him makes you feel?" Everything he says about feelings and
their articulation is intended to highlight or elucidate one or
other of these questions. The first question turns the person's
attention to the reality or unreality of the Lord's part in the
dialogue. The second addresses the reality or unreality of his
own part.

At the heart of dryness at this stage of prayer (the stage at
which no recognizable sense of sin has yet appeared) is a lack
of engagement in dialogue. The person does not listen or, if
he listens, he does not respond. He may say that he listens,
but hears nothing. Does he tell the Lord how he feels about
hearing nothing? Or he may say that the Lord knows what he
feels, so there is no reason to tell him. However, telling him
is not for the Lord's information, but for the sake of his own
openness, his personal engagement in dialogue.

When the person has tried to express what he feels to the
Lord, an exchange something like this may take place with
the director:

"Did you tell the Lord how you felt?"

"I didn't feel anything but confusion and frustration."

"Well, did you express the confusion and frustration to
him?"

The director will often find that the person does not readily
express such feelings in prayer. He believes them unworthy.
To him they are nonfacts, obstacles to be overcome so that

worthy feelings can eventually be placed before the Lord. So he tries to ignore them, tries not to notice them. As a result, he has nothing to say to the Lord.

Beneath the confusion and frustration often lurk other reactions even less acceptable to him. Anger at significant people in his life, resentment toward God, disappointment with himself, a sense of worthlessness may lie submerged in his consciousness. As he is called to speak "the whole truth" to the Lord, these feelings may threaten to emerge into awareness. But since they are unacceptable, he does not notice them, and as a result experiences confusion.

Unaccepted feelings can also come into consciousness obliquely. "I could feel very sad and discouraged about it, but that would be dumb." Because he feels sadness is improper, the person does not let himself notice that he is sad. Instead he reflects on the unreasonableness of being sad. The sadness, then, because it goes at least partly unnoticed, prevents him from listening to the Lord and responding to him. The director can help him by simply and repeatedly saying: "You're telling me how you think you should feel. But how *do* you feel?" Once he lets himself become aware of how he actually does feel, the person can begin to consider the sources and reasonableness of his sadness. Once he lets himself notice, he often finds that clear reflection on his feelings is both possible and helpful.

When such feelings are very strong, affective prayer is possible only if the person can put them before the Lord and let him accept them. Otherwise, the unnoticed negative feelings will stand like a ridge between him and the Holy One.

Now that an attempt has been made to describe the most obvious ways in which the directee can learn to notice inner facts, let us consider some examples of the kind of difficulty with prayer that most clearly indicates a need to notice.

Some people begin spiritual direction in a state of mild depression. They notice no sparkle, no color in life. Existence is a burden to be borne, a series of duties to be performed. When they try to pray, prayer, too, becomes a colorless duty. God's love and gifts seem faintly boring. This inner listlessness is not simply a result of objective burdens. A man under great pressure of work can enjoy some aspects of his work. A dying woman can enjoy the play of sunlight on a living-room rug. It will only be when a person begins to like and enjoy some of the gifts in his life, and notices that he does, that prayer can become an appreciative dialogue with a Giver who loves him. Until this happens, he may need a broader and more varied experience of life or other forms of pastoral care or counseling rather than frequent spiritual direction.

Others come for spiritual direction who persistently overlook disturbance or depression in their lives. They see disturbing and depressing events and conditions around them, but ignore the feelings these events arouse. They seem to need to be unfailingly cheerful, and in prayer always to feel that God is a comforting presence. If he rebukes them, or challenges them with sadness or conflict, they will not notice it because they feel they cannot afford to. God's action must be affirming, and prayer must be affirming. Spiritual directors, in their attempts to help them notice what is actually happening in prayer, will have to point to some of the feelings and conflicts they avoid. Otherwise prayer will exist disengaged from much of life, and because of this unreality will eventually become repellent to them.

Both these attitudes—unrelenting listlessness and dogged good cheer—have to yield to the realities of prayer and life if spiritual life is to grow and spiritual direction be helpful. Pointing repeatedly to discordant notes that sound in the prayer will usually be the most valuable assistance the director can give. But sometimes the person's defenses will be so entrenched that only a forthright confrontation will capture his attention. Such a confrontation would have to be focussed clearly on the main issue: Is he willing to notice what is happening in prayer and in his life, or is he screening out material that conflicts with a mood he feels he must maintain?

One of the most powerful inner facts is anger. When prayer flattens out, or appears to be facing an iron wall, the director must always suspect the presence of unexpressed anger. However, anger is socially unacceptable in our culture and our feelings enforce the social prohibition. So it tends to come out of hiding very reluctantly. Resentment, holding a grudge, or subdued rage, when they are present, are all likely to be given other names like hurt, indifference, and rational analy. is.

Not all anger, of course, will interfere with the recognition of one's spiritual identity. Hunger and thirst after justice for the Lord's people is hard to conceive of without anger, but anger which stems from love will further, not hinder, the dialogue with God. However, anger at what has happened to us, at the hurt we have sustained in our lives, is likely to be directed at the Source of our lives or at persons or institutions we emotionally associate with that Source. When this happens, anger often will block other affectivity and, until it is expressed to the Lord, will reduce prayer to rational reflection.

An analogy will help us understand how this happens. I am obliged to associate with someone who, I feel, has hurt me, disappointed me, perhaps betrayed my trust. I do not want to express my anger, perhaps because I am afraid of the person, perhaps because I feel that anger is always an unreasonable, unworthy reaction. How will I act when we meet? I may be affable, businesslike, or jocular, but because I do not want to expose myself to further hurt, I will keep my emotional distance. We can recognize this reaction readily when we recall instances of conscious anger. When, by hindsight, we also recall instances in which a subconscious anger was present, we can recognize that emotional distancing took place then, too, though we may not have understood the reason for it at the time.

A similar phenomenon takes place in the relationship with God. For it is the same "I" who relates to other human persons and to the Lord. He will not deal with me as humans do. "His love is everlasting." But my emotional reactions to him will be basically the same as the reactions I would have to human beings who affected my life as I feel God has. If I feel I have been hurt by life, I am likely to be as impervious to the Lord's overtures as I would be to the overtures of any man or woman who had hurt me. I will be resentful and afraid that I might be hurt again. If purposeful strength threatens and angers me, I will be disturbed by the purposeful strength of the Lord Jesus when his reality begins to impinge on my life.

As long as a person thinks of God as a set of propositions to be accepted intellectually, his prayer will not be particularly troubled by these reactions. But if, through a spiritual direction that opens to him the feasibility of living a contemplative attitude, he begins to realize that the living God is addressing him, he will begin to react, and his early reactions at least will follow the pattern he has been accustomed to when other persons who have affected his life in an analogous way have taken similar initiatives. This pattern will be at least partly subconscious, and so will be detected only if the directee continues to try to pray and notices what happens when he does.

When a person begins to notice the reactions that occur when he tries to pray, he has still another choice to make. This choice is often so spontaneously made that a person does not recognize it as a choice. It has, however, important consequences for his relationship with God. This is the choice to express or not to express his reactions to the Lord.

This expression is basically a sharing of oneself, and the decision to express is a decision not to keep one's affective life isolated from the Lord, but to share it with him, to some degree at least.

This sharing begins very simply with the first reaction a person notices when he begins to pray. "I was feeling that he wouldn't bother with me," a directee may say. "Everything

I had on my mind was so trivial. I wanted to skip praying just then. But I decided to tell him how I felt. I just said, 'I feel insignificant, worthless, too insignificant for you to pay attention. I don't even feel like paying attention to myself.' "

Sharing one's feelings is different from reporting feelings. "I feel O.K.," "I feel so-so," or "I feel fine," can be a beginning of sharing, but by themselves they communicate little to another person. If, however, a person wants to share his feelings, it will not be long before he becomes more explicit. "I feel O.K." can become "I even feel a little happy, pleased with the radiance of the sunlight"; "I feel so-so" can give way to "I feel dull . . . kind of sad"; "I feel fine" can give way to "I feel afraid of that examination I have scheduled for this afternoon."

A person who begins simply and wants to share his feelings will gradually find that he has deeper feelings to share. Desire and a willingness to let their feelings emerge are all that most people need to begin to share their feelings in prayer.

But isn't this introspective? Isn't it simply studying one's own inner workings? No more so than letting a close friend know exactly how one feels. Directees can tell the difference, if they reflect, between examining their feelings in order to know what they are and expressing them so that the other person can know them better and share their lives more explicitly.

How can a person tell whether he is reporting feeling or sharing it? People usually have some basis for comparison. They can remember instances of sharing feeling with other people and can recall the difference between those experiences and the reporting of feeling. As people become more accustomed to sharing reactions with the Lord, their deeper affective attitudes—their more basic desires, hopes, loves, fears, anger, guilt—begin to emerge into consciousness during prayer. If they can be content to share them rather than attempt to change them or suppress them as they begin to emerge, they find that their sense of relationship with the

Lord continues to grow in strength. They will not find the Lord a passive observer of their inner life. The relationship will no longer seem superficial.

An extended example may help us concretize the way a director can help a person notice his inner life. The conversation that follows can also help us see what can happen in prayer when a person notices his reactions and begins to share them with the Lord. In the description that follows, two directors (Dick and Ruth) with different approaches to spiritual direction listen and speak to the person who comes for direction.

Joe is a thirty-seven-year-old priest who has been seeing a spiritual director every two weeks for two months. During the conversation he recounts an incident that took place recently.

Joe: I had just come back from the funeral of the sister of a friend of mine, a woman in her early thirties who had died of cancer. She had been doing very well as a reporter for the local newspaper and had received several offers of work on larger papers in other parts of the country. Last year she received the journalism prize. The cancer was very swift and she died only a couple of months after finding out about it. I felt a little gloomy when I left the funeral. Frank, her brother, is a close friend of mine and it was pretty obvious that he was upset. Holding it in, but pretty hurt. When I got back to the house I picked up the Bible because I wanted to. I wanted to pray—I hadn't had a chance to pray during the day. And I turned to Psalm 139. I've used 139 very frequently but this time as I read about God probing me and knowing me, knowing my journeys and my resting places and shaping my life, I found myself getting more depressed. I had a few distractions and then became a little curious about what was happening because the distractions didn't concern things that were really of interest to me. I realized that I might be avoiding saying to the Lord what I really felt, so I addressed him. I found myself saying to him that he'd taken this woman who is doing very valuable work, living a good and happy life. And I found myself saying that he had taken my own sister, Agnes, just eight or nine months ago. There are a lot of people who live unhappy and not very productive lives, but Agnes hadn't been one of them. She'd been a happy woman who brought happiness to a lot of other people. Yet he had taken her. I had forgotten how strong and fresh my feelings still were.

Dick: This woman's funeral reminded you of your own sister's death?

Joe: It did.

Dick: I suppose the feelings of loss still haven't left you. That's normal enough, Joe. I didn't get over my own father's death for at least a year. You're probably still in the middle of the grief process.

Joe: I suppose I am. I hadn't realized it.

Dick: Well, you know, suffering loss is like suffering an illness. There isn't much you can do except give yourself time to recuperate.

Joe: Yes, I didn't particularly like the gloom. I don't like being gloomy. And especially I don't like still being gloomy about Agnes's death.

Ruth replies to Joe in a different way. After the description of the prayer she says:

Ruth: This woman's funeral reminded you of your sister's death?

Joe: It did.

Ruth: Did you address the Lord about that? You told him how you felt about his taking her?

Joe: Yes, I told him that I was still upset about it. After all these months. I was still upset. I told him I missed her, that she had brought a lot to my life. Told him that he had hurt me as well as her. I guess I felt a little selfish about saying that but I said it anyway.

Ruth: What did he seem like?

Joe: What do you mean?

Ruth: Was he there? Did you feel you were talking to yourself?

Joe: No, I didn't. I know what that talking-to-yourself feeling is like. I felt that he was there.

Ruth: Did you have any sense of what he was like?

Joe: I don't think so. Well, he was listening if that's saying something about what he was like. I suppose it is. He was listening. (Pause) He did not seem uninterested or unkind. He just seemed to listen.

Ruth: From far away?

Joe: I didn't have a sense of distance, or a sense of closeness for that matter. He was there. He was attentive. He heard me out.

Ruth: You kept telling him how you felt?

Joe: Yes, there was a lot. As I kept talking, I began to feel as though there was black bile in my stomach. That surprised me. That kind of bitterness is not usual with me. But there it was. I felt it about life and I felt it about God who after all is in charge of life. I said a lot. I didn't speak continuously, I paused a lot. But every few minutes I thought of something new I wanted to say.

Ruth: As you continued to speak to him, you kept on discovering more that you wanted to say to him?

Joe: Yes. I told him that sometimes he takes the best things in life, that Agnes had been a bright girl, never a gray or drab person, but a spark of brightness. A radiant person. I always felt alive after I talked to her. I told him that taking her was like putting out a light. I asked him why he had done that to me.

Ruth: Did he seem to be saying anything to you?

Joe: No.

Ruth: Was he still attentive?

Joe: Yes. And he didn't seem to move away. But there was no answer.

Ruth: How did that make you feel?

Joe: All right. Well, no. Angry. Angry that he wouldn't answer. That he would take a bright person like Agnes and wouldn't answer me.

Ruth: And he remained silent?

Joe: I kept on talking to him. I told him how drab my life is now. The way my work is going keeps leaving me discouraged, listless. I told him about that. And I told him that I don't know what I want to do next year. I don't know whether to continue with the chaplaincy or not.

Ruth: So you went on to tell him more about the way you feel about other aspects of your life?

Joe: Yes. He got a packet from me. I was surprised, I don't usually talk like that to the Lord. I guess I was surprised, too, that I had all that feeling.

Ruth: It turned out to be a lot of feeling.

Joe: Yes. And a lot of it came out.

Ruth: Did the black bile remain?

Joe: Funny, I don't remember it going. I wasn't conscious of it after awhile. I had been very conscious of it and for a fair amount of time. After awhile I wasn't aware of it anymore. I was aware of him listening and of a feeling of drabness about my life but not of the bile.

Ruth: Anything else happen in the prayer that you can recall, Joe?

Joe: No, nothing extraordinary. I did feel at the end that there was something good about the prayer.

Ruth: What did you think it was?

Joe: I'd come clean, I guess, and said things that were there unspoken. I'd gone ahead and said them. I hadn't edited what I was saying. I'm not sure I would have liked someone to be as uncontrolled as I was if he were speaking to me. But he had remained attentive.

Ruth: That had meant something to you?

Joe: It did. It meant that he took me seriously.

Both directors are knowledgeable people who wanted to help Joe. Neither wanted to avoid talking about his sister's death. The kinds of help they gave, however, are different and lead to different results in the conversation itself. More important, however, what Joe said to the two directors will probably affect differently the way he approaches God the next time he prays. Both directors have helped. But the kinds of help they gave will also have different effects on Joe's prayer.

In our examples, we have emphasized the indications that key facts can go unnoticed and the help that the director can give when he pays attention to these facts. It should be stressed, however, that every act of genuine noticing is the result of a free decision. The directee does not notice what he does not choose to notice. A spiritual direction based on the directee's willingness to notice becomes, then, a process of progressively greater openness to reality that is freely undertaken and freely pursued through a series of usually quiet, sometimes dramatic, decisions to see and not be blind.

6

Development of Relationship and Resistance

In his spiritual autobiography Thomas Merton recalls the summer when he heeded the call to go to Mass and began an extensive reading of Catholic literature. Then he says:

> And here is a strange thing. I had by now read James Joyce's *Ulysses* twice or three times. Six years before . . . I had tried to read *Portrait of the Artist* and had bogged down in the part about his spiritual crisis. Something about it had discouraged, bored and depressed me. I did not want to read about such a thing: and I finally dropped it in the middle of the "Mission." Strange to say, sometime during the summer . . . I reread *Portrait of the Artist* and was fascinated precisely by that part of the book, by the "Mission," by the priest's sermon on hell.[1]

The description of the early reading of *Portrait* gives a classic example of resistance to a further development in the relationship with God. He becomes "discouraged, bored, depressed" and gives up the reading which has brought on these feelings. If he had faced their source he might have recognized at that time the action of God that six years later enabled him to overcome his resistance and change his life style. But he was not ready for such a development, and so he put the book aside.

Relationships do not develop smoothly. There is something in us that resists change and development, that wants wives or husbands, friends, companions to be the same tomorrow as they are today. At the same time, there is something in us that wants to know more about the other and is bored by sameness. These two desires clash in us and produce conflict and resistance. Resistance is a critical element in the development of every interpersonal relationship. It does, therefore, play a part in the development of a relationship with God.

Traditional Christian teaching on spiritual life has often spoken of movements of the spirits.[2] In his Rules for the Discernment of Spirits,[3] Ignatius of Loyola describes characteristic movements of the "good spirit" and the "evil spirit." A major purpose of the "evil spirit" is to thwart the movement of the "good spirit" toward God. Our discussion of the development of relationship and resistance will approach some of the same phenomena from a contemporary perspective.

Discouragement, boredom, and depression surfaced in Merton as he read *Portrait*. These feelings are signs of the presence of resistance in a person. Prayer can be attractive and absorbing for a while, and then, sometimes quite abruptly, go dull and tasteless. The person praying feels that nothing is happening, gets discouraged, and wonders whether the prior experiences of closeness to God were chimerical, the product of his own desires and fantasy. He begins to focus on himself and his problems when he tries to pray. He also tends to avoid prayer.

A constantly cheery, emotionally unnuanced experience of prayer can also be a sign of resistance. Real relationships are never smooth sailing for long. Blindness to certain facets of life or to the obvious meaning of a text of Scripture is a manifestation of resistance. For instance, a Christian social activist who has just read the first ten chapters of Mark might be startled when he is told that Mark twice mentions that Jesus went aside to pray. He goes back to the text to make sure it mentions these incidents, and then comes to realize that his blindness signals resistance to developing his own prayer life.

Resistance also manifests itself in persistent repetition of the same pattern of response. For example, a woman takes several instances of healing miracles in the gospels for prayer and repeatedly accuses herself of lacking faith, of not being humble enough. Weeks of praying for healing and growth produce no change. The pattern has kept her from noticing the love of Jesus for the sick and needy people he meets and thus for herself.

Falling asleep in prayer can be a sign of extreme tiredness, but it also can be an instance of massive resistance to meeting the Holy One. One woman was desirous of a closer relationship with Jesus yet found herself falling asleep in prayer, something that had not happened since college. As she and the director explored what was going on, it became clear that for her conversation with Jesus meant a radical departure from her past life. Before this abyss the only solution was to avoid looking.

Doubts about the reality of prayer and the possibility of ever knowing whether one has experienced God can be manifestations of resistance. Avoidance of prayer and of appointments with the spiritual director, repeated lateness for appointments, discussions with the director of everything but prayer experience, desires to quit direction, all can be signs of the presence of resistance to the Lord.

The ways resistance will show itself are probably only limited by the ingenuity of the person praying. The relationship with God is dynamic; hence the ubiquity of resistance in prayer and spiritual direction. If directors are not prepared to encounter this tendency, they themselves may become dismayed, discouraged, or angry. It will be helpful, we believe, for directors to understand how relationships in general develop and how resistance is a part of that process.

Forming and developing any genuine close relationship makes demands on a person's deepest resources of heart and mind. The demand is no less rigorous when one of the two in the relationship is the mysterious Other we call God. Even when the two persons are human and thus visible, accurate perception of one another is difficult. How does one know the reality of the other person and of oneself? Not only do our categories and feelings organize our experience of others, they also organize our presentation of ourselves to others. How does such organization affect relationships?

The organization of interpersonal experience follows the general laws of the organization of any experience. Human beings never experience things in the raw, that is, without some organization of that experience by the experiencing person. Modern communication and information theory is built on the premise that communication of a message occurs only insofar as the recipient is ready to receive it. We can only assimilate what we have some expectation of receiving from a communication. I cannot assimilate a message in a language I do not understand because I have no way of organizing that experience. The dictum of the scholastic philosophers, "whatever is received is received according to the manner or nature of the recipient," has been modernized and made applicable to a wide range of events by communication theory.

The structuring or organizing of experience which we all do is based on our past experience and on what we have learned from that experience. Thus, our perceptions are influenced both by what we have already perceived and by what we expect to see. Our perceptions, therefore, can be systematically distorted by our expectations. Long before the Copernican revolution in Europe, for example, Chinese astronomers saw new stars which European astronomers did not see although both looked at the same heavens with roughly comparable instruments. The cosmological beliefs of the Chinese "did not preclude celestial change" and so they had expectations of finding "new" stars. The Ptolemaic cosmology of the Europeans did preclude the possibility of such change. They expected that they would not see anything new, and they did not.[4]

Moreover, evidence that runs counter to our expectations is at first resisted and, indeed, causes at least some anxiety. The history of science offers many examples of how events that run counter to expectations (that is, anomalies) are either not seen, or are treated as measuring errors or as problems to be solved by further experiment (thereby leaving expectations untouched). Psychological experiments also demonstrate how we avoid seeing the unexpected and are made anxious by it when it forces itself on our attention.[5] Something that does not fit our expectations is inexplicable, at least at first, and our immediate reaction is to try to fit the novelty into some category we are familiar with. "We tolerate the unexplained but not the inexplicable."[6]

Generally speaking, we are unaware of the structures we use to organize our experience. We are aware of what we see, but not of how we structure or interpret what we see. Moreover, we resist becoming aware of the structuring we do because that awareness would open us to the realization that we are structuring or framing our reality with the consequent question of whether we are in contact with the real at all. For the most part, we need not become aware because our expectations are met by events. Anomalies that force themselves on our attention can, however, make us aware that we have been structuring our experience in ways that precluded our perception of certain realities. Under these circumstances we can become aware of our structuring propensities. It hardly need be said that structuring is a necessity, not something we can do without.

In the realm of interpersonal experience expectations play a significant role. On the basis of our experiences with other people, we each build up within ourselves expectations (the technical term is schemata[7]) of how we will look to others and they to us. These expectations are personality patterns for organizing our experience with other people. As with any other personality structure, these, too, are generally not adverted to and in this sense operate unconsciously. Every new person we meet is assimilated to one or other of these self-other schemata, and we have initial positive, negative, ambivalent, or neutral reactions toward the new person and toward ourselves depending on which one is activated. Hopefully our expectations are flexible and differentiated enough to accommodate the novelty and individuality of the stranger. Whether they actually are or not will depend on our early positive experiences with significant people and on the variety and quality of experiences we have had with people throughout our lives.

A very simplified example may help in understanding the last point. A man who has had a highly ambivalent relationship with his mother might have only two categories for assimilating women who enter his life: loving and yielding or hating and demanding. Whenever he meets a woman for the first time, he reacts to her as one or the other; he is attracted if she seems loving and yielding, repelled if she seems the opposite. Real women, even if loving, are more nuanced than this and so quickly shun his company. So this man does not have extensive enough relationships with women to find out that there might be other categories. His images of women never change, nor, of course, does his own image of himself.

Every unexpected event, all unexpected behavior, every stranger causes some anxiety, some disquiet. If that anxiety is minimal (because the novelty is insignificant), then no accommodation is necessary and no new learning about self and others in relationship takes place. If the anxiety is very severe, then there can be a regression to an earlier and less mature way of coping (when, for example, a soldier terrified in battle begins to whimper and cry for his mother) or a fixation at a child's developmental level of personality pattern (as in the example of the man who sees women only as yielding or demanding). A moderate amount of anxiety appears to be a necessary stimulus for growth and development; if we never experienced novelty, we would never change.[8] If a relationship is to develop, then each of the parties has to be open to letting the novelty and mystery of the other shake the patterning of the relationship that has developed from prior experience. Thus, each has to be open to experiencing some anxiety.

But there is also an inertial tendency in every personality

pattern that resists change. Since these patterns organize experience, change means—or seems to mean—the disorganization of experience. We fear chaos. Self-other schemata organize our interpersonal experience and give a sense of continuity to our images of self and others. A shake-up in the image of oneself or of an intimate and/or significant other can threaten a person at a rather profound level. These images also have roots in childhood experience where the difference between order and chaos was rather slender. Their disturbance, even in a mature person, can bring back those early feelings of vulnerability. Hence, we can understand the resistance to change and the anxiety that can occur even when the novelty is only dimly perceived.

It is important to remember that these patterns or images organize both our experience of others and our experience of ourselves. Thus, the way we see ourselves in interaction with others is involved. Part of the change that must occur if an intimate relationship is to develop is a change of the self-image, at least in relationship with this intimate person. As I allow the other to be different from my expectations and thus more himself, so, too, I allow myself to be different from my "ideal self" and thus more transparent to him. When relationships are allowed to develop, more of oneself and of the other is revealed, and each becomes better able to influence and change the other's personality patterns. Each takes on for the other a life and a personality that is independent of that other's expectations, and in the process each takes on for himself a life and personality freed of at least some of the constraints of his own self-image.

Benign shake-ups of these patterns occur in the context of a trusted and loving relationship. If the basis of the relationship is relatively solid, then the unexpected is more readily accepted and accommodated.[9] This fact should motivate the spiritual director to make every effort to help the directee establish as soon as possible a deep and abiding trust in God. For many people the establishment of such trust is not easy.

Even when early relationships have been healthy, and flexible and differentiated personality patterns have developed and are developing, still, for many people the images for self and for God have not been given a chance to develop. Many people, in other words, live with an image of their relationship with God that is childish or juvenile, not because of any traumatic events in their lives, but because they never had a chance or took the opportunity to engage the Lord in a relationship that matured as they matured. The establishment of trust will be even more difficult where the self-God image is also mired in a fixated child-parent image.

Directees will need much help at the beginning to let God enter their lives in a real relationship if their images are undeveloped. At this stage they need encouragement to look and listen, to allow their desires for a more mature and trusting relationship to surface, to allow their angry and disappointed feelings to surface as well. This is no time to focus on sin, since all such a focus can do is lead to self-absorption and continued fixation. Resistance will occur at this stage too, and the resistance may be quite strong because the directee may feel that the alternative to his self-God image is a self-alone image; that is, the person may feel that he will lose God altogether. The only image of God such a person knows is the childish or juvenile one, and to face giving that one up may seem like facing atheism or agnosticism. Such a prospect can be very anxiety-provoking and bring on strong resistance to the process.

We will not dwell on the vicissitudes of the self-God image and its developmental history. That is a task for a developmental religious psychology.[10] The relationship with God is conditioned by such an image or schema just as is any other relationship. Thus, one will tend to present oneself to God on the basis of what one imagines is the "right way" to relate to God, and one will tend to experience God in the way one expects to experience him. Any novelty—either in one's own self-presentation or in the presentation of God—will provoke at least some anxiety and some resistance and may indeed go unnoticed at first precisely because it is unexpected. Finally, only continued contact with God and commitment to the relationship with him and to attempts at openness will change one's image of God and oneself in relationship.

Indeed, since God is *semper maior*—always greater—one can expect that relating to him will mean being open to continuous novelty and thus continuous change of images. Spiritual idolatry could be seen as unwillingness to let God be other than one's present image of him. For example, the scrupulous person holds an image of God as tyrant and cannot or will not let God change that image and thus free him of his scruples. Faith, then, would move us to let him break out of every image, to try to overcome our resistance to such a shake-up of our images, to live with the Mystery we call God—*and* with the anxiety of not being able finally to organize that experience of him in such a way as to make him merely unexplained rather than inexplicable. The openness to such an ever-greater God must rest on the firm foundation of a basic sense of trust that probably can come only from the enjoyment of God.

> The *enjoyment of God* should be the supreme end of spiritual technique; and it is in that enjoyment of God that we feel not only saved in the Evangelical sense, but safe; we are conscious of belonging to God, and hence are never alone. . . . In that relationship Nature seems friendly and homely; even its vast spaces instead of eliciting a sense of terror speak of the infinite love; and the nearer beauty becomes the garment with which the Almighty clothes Himself. [11]

An experience like this seems to be necessary as a foundation for the development of the relationship.

A universal source of resistance is, then, personality structure itself. All structures are essentially conservative. They are also necessary to us; without them experience would be meaningless and chaotic. Perhaps because of the threat of chaos, structures tend to resist change. Or rather, we structured people tend to resist change. Spiritual direction, with its purpose of facilitating relationship with an ever-greater God, opposes this conservative tendency and can, therefore, expect to evoke resistance. Indeed, lack of resistance to prayer and to spiritual direction is a warning sign that the direction and the prayer are on the wrong track. Resistance in prayer is not something to be condemned or pitied but rather welcomed as an indication that the relationship with God is broadening and deepening. Let us look at some specific sources of resistance.

The fear that one will lose the relationship with God has been mentioned as one major source of resistance. The obverse side of this fear of losing God is the fear that I will lose myself, that I will be swallowed up in the immensity of God. Whatever the ultimate source—whether it is fear of the awesomeness of God or a reflection of the fact that our self-God image ultimately rests on the earliest self-other images, where self-other boundaries were very fragile—some resistance does seem to stem from a fear that the person will lose himself if he lets God enter his experience in a new way. A healthy, active, though shy woman, after a few weeks of very consoling prayer in which she feels God extremely close to her, begins to say to herself, "This is too high-falutin for me." and goes back to a more prosaic kind of prayer that consists in planning how she will serve God and her family better. That she is resisting becomes clear when the more prosaic prayer leaves her confused and self-preoccupied. The contemplative attitude can be particularly frightening in such circumstances because it seems to ask one to give up control. Thus there will often be a movement away from contemplation, which can manifest itself in the fear that one is being presumptuous.

Another source of resistance is the particular self-God image a person has. Many people have an image that prevents them from expressing mean, angry, jealous, resentful, or sexual feelings to God. They will therefore resist any process that threatens to evoke such reactions in prayer. The contemplative attitude is such a process, since it asks that the contemplative let his responses be elicited by what he perceives—and some things he perceives may evoke the "bad" feelings. For example, contemplating the scene[12] in which Jesus visits the home of Martha and Mary and Martha does all the work may evoke in a person jealous and hostile feelings of being put upon by others, feelings that the person finds unworthy of prayer. The person will tend to avoid this scene and may replace contemplation itself with rote prayers or the use of a prayer book.

Many people seem to relate to God as though he were someone who cannot abide pleasure or happiness in them. For them the idea of surrender to the process of contemplative prayer evokes fears that God will pummel them with demands for abnegation. They resist such surrender with vigor.

Still another source of movement that runs counter to God is the image of God as eternal, timeless, changeless, all-knowing, and cold. "How can I relate warmly to such a God?" "Why do I need to tell him everything since he knows it all already?" Such attitudes can block the development of the relationship. Alternatively, a directee may become frightened that prayer is leading into heresy or idolatry because God does seem to change.

In the middle stages of spiritual direction when the question of following Jesus more closely arises, resistance may spring from much more realistic fears. The rich young man in Mark's gospel[13] provides one example. The same gospel also provides another. Jesus three times talks in detail about his coming passion.[14] The disciples are concerned about who will be the greatest and as a result of their ambition seem unable to hear what Jesus is saying. As if to underline their resistance, Mark places one cure of a blind man a few lines before the first prediction[15] and another a few lines after the third prediction.[16] The man or woman who wants to follow Jesus closely may well, like these apostles, be afraid of the consequences of that desire. Here the resistances are more subtle and may well masquerade as angels of light. Once again, however, the resistances will appear in some form of a self-God image that imprisons God. The image may betray itself in a phrase like, "God can't ask the impossible of a person," a statement that is true but that can also mask resistance to a God who asks self-sacrificing love. Ignatius of Loyola speaks of "fallacious reasonings" as one of the movements of the evil spirit when his sole purpose, it seems, is to stall movement toward discipleship.[17].

While the main purpose of spiritual direction is to facilitate the relationship between the Lord and the directee, and while, therefore, the hope of the director is that the source and focus of resistances will be concentrated in that relationship, it must still be expected that the relationship between director and directee will also be a source of resistance. This relationship, too, will be conditioned by self-other images and so will be liable to distortion by both parties.[18]

It is important when discussing resistance to recall that directees have deliberately put themselves into a situation where they will experience it. There is, in other words, something in the directee that impels him toward growth in the relationship with God. Call it the desire for more life or the desire for more meaning, an impulse toward transcendence is there. The Spirit dwelling in the hearts of those who seek spiritual direction gives them the courage to stay with the process even when the journey is hard and resistance is strong. Directors can count on this Spirit and the impetus he gives. While resistance is a constant factor to be reckoned with in spiritual direction, the drive toward transcendence is also a constant. To paraphrase St. Paul: ". . . but where resistance increased grace abounded all the more. . . ."[19]

As we have previously said, the kind of structuring of experience we have been discussing generally goes on without our awareness. By the same token, resistance is more successful when it goes unnoticed. People may consciously resist processes, of course, but the resistance we have here described usually operates unconsciously or semiconsciously. If directors are to help directees overcome resistance, they must first recognize its presence. This means that they must pay attention to what is happening to directees and know the signs of resistance.

The contemplative attitude of directors toward those they direct will be of great help here. For their first concern must be to see and hear the directee and to respond to him rather than to their own preoccupations. Directors who adopt a contemplative way of approaching directees seek to become more focussed on the other person, unhampered in their view by biases and preferences, and aware at the same time of their emotional reactions to the conversation.

Besides noticing the signs of resistance we mentioned earlier, directors can look to their own reactions for signals that might indicate the presence of resistance in the directee. If a director finds himself getting bored or irritable, he may be reacting to a resistive directee who is actually boring or irritating. He needs to know, of course, that he is not projecting his own problems onto the directee. Directors can also make use of the general criteria for evaluating religious experience which we will discuss in the next chapter. They ought not, however, see themselves as detectives hunting down clues to crime. Resistance is no crime, but a necessary concomitant to any effort at growth. Directors are collaborators with the directee, and they hope that the directee, as a result of his experience, will begin to notice his own resistances for himself.

The next question is: What do directors do once they notice resistance or countermovements? First of all, they must keep their sense of humor and an awareness of their own fallibility. The signs of resistance are only that—signs, not proof.

Before resistance is confronted and uncovered, there should be a good working alliance[20] between director and directee. If there is not, the confrontation will probably not lead to an overcoming of the resistance, but to a hardening of it. For the confrontation will be experienced by the directee as an attack, even as a humiliation. The danger, then, is that an adversary relationship will ensue. Timing is important; a directee can easily explain away a single instance of resistance. It is wise to let the resistance develop before confronting it, so that a number of instances can be used to point out a resistive pattern.

Here is an illustration of a director helping a directee to notice a pattern of movement and countermovement. The directee (Jean) is a married church worker and has been in direction for a few months. The director (Joe) has noticed himself becoming bored and irritated during their meetings, and these feelings have prompted him to reflect back over the course of the direction. He has recalled that there have been several intense experiences of the Lord's closeness, each followed by a lengthy period of distractions and concerns about work. He decides to confront the directee in this meeting if it seems appropriate. The exchange goes something like this:

Jean: Prayer's been one round of distractions, really; home, work, the church—they all just crowd in. And I'm just so busy; there's no time really.

Joe: You know, it might be a good idea if we could take a look together at just what has been happening the last couple of months while you've been seeing me.

Jean: That could be a good idea.

Joe: How do you see it, Jean? I know you enjoy our exchanges, but there's more to it than that, isn't there?

Jean: Well, I wanted a deeper, closer relationship with the Lord and I'm seeing that in a wider context of the family, the church, and work, bringing him into all those areas. That's what's been happening.

Joe: I think I see it in a somewhat more detailed way. I was very moved a couple of months ago when you shared your experience of hearing the Lord say to you, "My daughter"—You remember that? (Jean nods and brightens). You were going to go back to that, and you were going to talk to the Lord about your relationship with your own father. That intention seemed to fade, though. Then there was your experience of Jesus as friend. That was very strong. After that, time with the Lord seemed to get crowded out. You were going to pray over the choices you felt you were faced with and you talked about your own riches and following the Lord. Some of these have been pretty important issues for you, but you've never followed through with any of them.

Jean: That's very true.

Joe: What stops you, Jean?

Jean: I'm scared, really, afraid I might find out I'm not the sort of person I'd like to be. I'm really afraid.

Joe: What's the worst that might happen?

Jean: I'd find out I'm pretty worthless and incompetent and I'd run away.

Joe: How would you feel if you did?

Jean: I don't know; pretty ashamed, I guess.

Joe: How do you think the Lord would feel?

Jean: Oh, I just need to hear him say "My daughter, your sins are forgiven. . . ."

This is a good illustration of what we have just been discussing. The director has obviously been paying attention to the directee and has a good working relationship with her. He has also paid attention to what was happening inside himself and as a result took some time to reflect on the sessions of the past few months. He noted a pattern, and he presented it to Jean in such a way that she could see it and reflect on it and realize that the countermovement was motivated by fear of her worthlessness. The way the director points to the pattern is important. He does not accuse, but rather invites her to look at what has been happening. "It seems that you're having trouble talking about prayer today" is a better approach than "You're avoiding talk about prayer." The first invites the directee to consider a possible difficulty and indicates that today is different from other days; the second is an assertion that could lead the directee to take a stronger defensive position.

The director wants the directee to reflect on what he sees as happening and makes it clear by his manner that he and she are collaborators in this enterprise. If the directee asks him what gave the impression she was having trouble, he points out the signs he has noticed. If she denies his conclusion, he does not try to argue but might say something like "It was a possibility I thought might be good to test out with you." If she is resisting, there will be more and more indications of it, and it will eventually become obvious to both. The director has not made his view of things the focus, but has kept the focus on her prayer and her presentation of her experiences in prayer. Patience is necessary, as is trust in the process of contemplative prayer and in the working alliance he has with the directee. If there is resistance, it will show itself in prayer by the appearance of a greater and greater distance of the Lord from the directee. The director can patiently point to this and other evidence and trust that eventually the directee herself will see that something is wrong.[21]

In the illustration Jean made a rather stunning statement. She said that she wanted "a closer, deeper relationship with the Lord." Many directees say the same thing. Do most people who say this really mean that they want to relate more closely with "the Lord of heaven and earth," the *mysterium tremendum*? The comment of a woman of an earlier generation who heard a statement like this seems more credible: "In my time we wanted to be on the right side of him, but we didn't want to get too close." The humor such a remark evokes should not hide the fact that such an attitude has deep roots in us, roots that are, perhaps, as deep as the desire for closeness.

One of the notable advantages of a spiritual direction that emphasizes a directee's freedom is that it respects the depth and tenacity of these roots. This depth shows itself in the strength of the movements that keep a person like Jean from advancing further in her relationship with God. These roots show themselves with particular tenacity as she comes closer to opening herself more significantly to God's action or to revealing herself in a fuller transparency. The resistance can become strong enough so that people remain on the same level of closeness to him for months, often for years. During this time the relationship with God may operate with freedom on the level it has reached but, despite recurrent invitations from the Lord to move deeper, it stays there.

The level at which the development stops and remains may be the level on which a person can speak freely to God about much of his activity and some of his motivation, but cannot express some of his deeper and more sheltered feelings, for example, a confusion that shows itself only infrequently and that concerns his conviction or lack of conviction about the worth of his life. Another example would be a doubt seldom adverted to by a minister about his desire to continue in pastoral work. Another might be a deep anger at the circumstances of one's early life, particularly when this anger relates to persons who are dear to one.

Still another level of fixation occurs when the person can look at God's action but not respond to that action with more than superficial feeling. A woman knows, for example, from her experience, that Jesus has acted toward her in a way in which only very close friends act. He has sacrificed, for example, his own good for her sake. She can respond with thanks but not with the deeper resources of her heart: profound caring, troubled feelings at the mediocrity of the way she shares the mission of Jesus, deep feelings of loyalty, and chagrin at the predicament of his people.

No one can be forced to go beyond the level at which he is fixated. Directors do as much as they can at this point when they help the person look at, recognize, and experience the reality of the level on which he lives. In this way the directee has an opportunity to see the reality of his life and measure it against his desires—and particularly against any invitations he may be receiving to go deeper. The woman, for example, who is thankful to Jesus for his self-sacrifice and many acts of generosity toward her, but who cannot let the deeper resources of her heart enter into that gratitude, can perhaps best be helped by a director who is willing to encourage her to keep looking at the action of Jesus in her regard, at the reality of her gratitude, and at the point at which that gratitude ceases to touch her. Pushing her to go deeper would usually not be a help to her and might well strengthen her guilt at not going deeper. Drawing her to concentrate on that guilt might well lead her away from attention to the invitation of the Lord and the possibilities of response that are open to her.

For a person in this situation of fixation much of the language of traditional spirituality is not helpful. He can say, "I should give everything to the Lord." Or he may keep trying to make his own a prayer of total giving he has found in a prayer book. The words he uses are words of total generosity and represent what he feels his attitude toward the Lord should be. They do not, however, represent his actual state and the choices that are open to him at this moment. Those choices generally represent the possibility of moving an inch. If his attention is fixed by the language of his prayer on the infinite distance he feels he should travel, he may not recognize that he can move an inch. Or, if he does recognize it, he may not take the choice seriously. The director who has worked out ways of respecting both a person's freedom and God's freedom will be willing to allow the person to stop his development of openness to God at the point at which he comes to live with a modicum of peace, if that is what the person wants at that time. He will not think of him as a weakling because he knows that desire to go further may not be present now but may well emerge after a period of pause in his development. Circumstances may appear that will serve as a catalyst for greater desire. God can act in a new way at any time. Respect for these facts is probably a genuine respect for the necessity and the goodness of the person's desire itself. One of the purposes of direction thus becomes the effort to help a person see the reality or nonreality of his expression of his desires while making sure that no judgment is placed on the configuration or force of those desires.

What do director and directee do about resistance when

they discover it? One extreme would be to adopt the psychoanalyst's approach and try to uncover all the motives and history behind this particular resistance, a type of archaeology of the spirit. The other extreme would be to exhort the directee to "take it to the Lord" without any further discussion. A middle ground might be more profitable for the directee and yet possible for the director. It would be helpful for the directee to come to know the ambivalence of his own desires through reflection on the resistance. He would thus recognize that he is caught between two conflicting desires and could appeal to the Lord for help in overcoming the ambivalence in favor of his desire to know the Lord better. In other words, he could be helped to sharpen the focus of his desires; where before he was, perhaps, asking to experience the closeness of God, now he knows that he wants to ask for help to overcome the fear of that closeness.

It would also help if the directee were to see the resistance as part of a pattern in his life and prayer. For example, the ambivalence we just mentioned might be evident in a number of his relationships and in his attitude toward ministry, and he may be enabled to focus his desire for God's help on all these areas. In this way prayer and life would come together. We are suggesting, in other words, that the director who has worked for some time with a directee may be able to help him see one instance of resistance as part of a larger pattern in his life and thus help him bring more of himself before the Lord for help. At any rate, the major point is that a resistance uncovered means that the directee has something new to talk to the Lord about, and each such resistance uncovered leads to more and more reality in the relationship. The Lord is allowed to be more transparent and the directee lets himself be more transparent.

One particular form of resistance deserves comment and raises an issue that needs study. Resistances often crystallize around some kind of secret: There is something I don't want the Lord, or my director—or frequently enough, myself—to know about. The resistance begins to occur when the "secret" gets close to the surface of awareness. Obviously there is no way around the difficulty; the secret must eventually be shared with the Lord. There is sometimes a question as to whether it is also necessary to tell it to the director in order to overcome the resistance and move along smoothly with the direction. We have known instances where it was first necessary for the person to be able to tell the director the secret before he could tell it to the Lord. We also know instances in which the secret was shared with the Lord and not with the director. In these cases, however, it seemed that the director needed to help the directee recognize that the "secret" was blocking progress in prayer and thus help him tell the whole truth to God. The direction did not seem to suffer from withholding the secret from the director. It may even be that this withholding reinforced the primacy of the relationship between God and the directee. The conclusion, however, needs to be kept in perspective. The directee, once he can speak of the secret at all, usually reveals it spontaneously to both the Lord and the director. We also recall Ignatius of Loyola's experienced voice saying that "the enemy of our human nature . . . earnestly desires that they (his wiles and seductions) be received secretly and kept secret," and urging manifestation to a confessor or "spiritual person."[22]

Several other remarks may be helpful to directors. When resistance or a countermovement occurs, it is usually necessary to note and reflect on that movement before looking at the reasons for it. Jean first had to recognize that there was a pattern of approach-avoidance before she could be helped to look at the reasons for it. The woman who thought that the profoundly consoling prayer she experienced was too highfalutin' for her needed first to see the possibility that she was resisting before she and the director could profitably look at some of the meaning of her fear. If the director had immediately said that it sounded as though she was afraid of loss of self or had a low opinion of herself, she might well have agreed verbally, but probably would have been unable to do anything with the knowledge except go further into self-absorption. It seems that resistance or countermovement needs to be uncovered first and contemplated before director and directee can work on content or meaning.

It also seems advisable to start at the surface—the director begins where the person is most aware of difficulty. Spiritual directors have to be wary of offering profound interpretations of another's spiritual experience. Their primary task is to begin where the other is and help him move further.

Obviously spiritual directors, like everyone else, have their anxieties and fears and their categories for self-other relationships. Like people learning the practice of any profession, when they are beginning direction they will be anxious to do the "right" thing, to ask the "right" questions, to use the "right" words, and may not pay enough attention to the directee. It may not be amiss, at this point, to say a cautionary word about our use of language and our tendency to impose our suppositions on the directee. "Resistance," "schema," "self-other images," as well as "first week," "consolation," "grace," and many other terms are technical language. Directors should use direct and nontechnical words with people. Thus, it seems preferable to say: "You seem to be avoiding something, or having a hard time describing your experience," or "You sound sad, or angry, or depressed," or "How did you feel about those words of Jesus?" Secondly, if a director has come to a new insight, he may be eager to "clarify some things" for the directee. As a result, he may not let the directee determine how the session will begin, and he may not listen well. Directors should be careful not to let their own agenda get in the way of their contemplative attitude.

Criteria for Evaluating Religious Experience

In ancient Israel there were both true and false prophets. In New Testament times there were conflicting parties, each claiming that it taught the authentic doctrine of Jesus. Throughout history men and women who asserted that they knew what God wanted have been proved wrong by events. As a result the Church has traditionally been wary of private revelation. How then can anyone know whether he is hearing God or is suffering delusion? Can his relationship with God help him to make choices?

Several times in the last three chapters we have given examples of people noticing something in their prayer and making decisions on the basis of what they have noticed. In one instance a man noticed that the black bile of his anger had disappeared and was convinced that the Lord had heard him out. In another instance a woman recognized a pattern of approach and avoidance in her prayer and decided that fear was keeping her at a distance from the Lord. Such decisions are made frequently in prayer and spiritual direction, and people seem able to make them with relative ease. How do they make these decisions? What kind of criteria do they use? These people are "discerning the spirits." How do they do it?

Much of the literature of discernment, especially in the Ignatian tradition, speaks of ways of finding God's will in the choice of a state of life. People's experience, however, indicates that the habit of discernment must begin long before a person makes such a momentous choice. It indicates, too, that discernment is a simple process, though not always an easy one. An example from the experience of the Desert Fathers, celebrated in Christian tradition for the earthy astuteness of their discernment, points out this simplicity.

One monk approaches another with a question: "I have an obligation," he says, "to give money that I earn to the poor. Now my sister, too, is poor. Isn't it all the same if I give my earnings to her rather than to other poor people?"

The second monk says, "No."

The first asks, "Why not?"

The other replies, "Because blood is thicker than water."[1]

We notice that the second monk does not offer exhortation or admonition. He contents himself with answering the question. The result of the discussion is that the questioner gets an opportunity to avoid confusing two different situations.

Discernment at its most basic level consists of recognizing differences. In the *Autobiography*, Ignatius of Loyola gives an extended description of his first experience of discernment. When he dreamed of doing knightly exploits and of winning the hand of a great lady, he felt happy and enthusiastic. But the feelings of happiness were later replaced by a feeling of discontent. When he dreamed of doing great things for God, he again felt happy and enthusiastic. This happiness, however, persisted. After some time, he says, "his eyes were opened a little, and he began to marvel at the difference and to reflect upon it, realizing from experience that some thoughts left him sad and others happy."[2] He had taken the first step that led him to a lifetime of distinguishing what was of God from other, potentially misleading, impulses.

If we recognize that discernment is, finally, nothing more than being able to recognize and admit differences, we can appreciate both its simplicity and its value. We can also realize that directors are helping people discern when they help them notice what is going on as they pray.

But we still need to ask what criteria can be used to decide on the authenticity or inauthenticity of experiences of God in prayer and in life generally. Not all spiritual experiences are from the Lord. We can be so delighted to break loose from preoccupation with routine and from deadening habits of rational prayer that we can prize every experience that involves affective response to a harmony and tranquility beyond our ordinary apprehension. However, there are experiences of harmony and tranquility that do not open us to God, but rather bring to a halt—at least temporarily—our movement toward him.

For example, a person who has steadily become more deeply aware of Jesus as desiring companionship with him may, in prayer, have an experience of an abstract, impersonal beauty that fascinates him. Unless he recognizes that there is a difference in the quality of his response to the Lord that takes place in these two experiences and asks himself whether he wants to continue with the experience of Jesus, he may well, without thinking about it, concentrate for days or weeks on the new experience precisely because it is an attractive spiritual experience.

In the *Autobiography*, Ignatius tells us that something like this happened to him. He often saw in the air before him a beautiful image that gave him great comfort. "It seemed to him to have the form of a serpent with many things that shone like eyes, though they were not eyes. He found great pleasure and consolation in seeing this thing, and the more he saw it the more his consolation increased. When it disappeared he was saddened."[3] Immediately after the experience of God at the river Cardoner, while kneeling in front of a crucifix, he saw the image again. This time, however, he noticed "that the object did not have its usual beautiful color, and with a strong affirmation of his will he knew very clearly that it came from the demon."[4]

Here we see one of the criteria that people use to decide whether an experience is of God: They compare it to another experience that they are sure is of God. Then, if they see that in some respect the two conflict, they decide which experience to accept. Many people have a touchstone experience of God. Any other experience that seems to run counter to that touchstone they look upon with suspicion. God can be so manifestly present to them during such a touchstone experience that they cannot doubt it any more than they can doubt their own existence.

The quality of the dialogue with God in prayer can also serve as a criterion for discernment. When, for example, we prematurely discontinue a dialogue we have begun with a person, the discontinuation may have significance for the relationship. Often enough we tend to explain such a choice by referring to circumstances extraneous to the relationship; for example, "I was tired and overworked," or "I was just feeling angry at the world." We need also, however, to be aware of possible reasons within the relationship itself; for example, "I didn't want to talk to her last night because she had hurt me." When we look at the quality of our dialogue with God from the same point of view, the results can be illuminating. Blandness in speaking to the Lord, for instance, can imply a desire to keep him at an emotional distance as it often does in other relationships. If we ask ourselves, "What is it that makes me want to be distant just now?," the answer may be: "I want to speak to the Lord, but I don't want to tell him what I'm feeling," or "I'm afraid of what he will say."

If a person has had the experience of an engaging, vital dialogue with the Lord in prayer, when the Lord and he both seemed present and expressive, then he can use this experience as a comparison point when the dialogue becomes dull and the Lord seems distant. Often enough, such dullness and distance occur because important affective attitudes are not being expressed.

It is frequently quite easy for a person to recognize that he can move from a dull dialogue to a much more varied and colorful one by expressing feelings that he is aware of. Sometimes, however, the person is not aware of the feelings that are there to be expressed. A director can then be helpful by asking: "Do you remember the last time that prayer was exciting or interesting for you? What were you talking about?" And then: "What happened to that topic?" Often the person recognizes that prayer went dull when a topic came up between the Lord and himself, and he chose not to pursue it. The prayer will remain dull until he comes back to that topic. When he does, the change from dullness to new interest is often dramatic.

This characteristic of the dialogue with God in prayer can keep prayer firmly linked to the dialogue with God in life outside prayer. If a man is troubled by the way his wife and he are interacting, for example, and yet does not permit himself even to advert to the trouble in prayer, he may well find that his prayer is boring. The prayer, in other words, lets him know that he is not being himself with the Lord. Attention to the quality of the dialogue with the Lord helps us discern where we may be blinding ourselves to the light in our lives.

Thus, one of the major criteria for the authenticity of our prayer and our lives is: "Is the dialogue working?" In other words, "Do I have something to say to the Lord that means something to me? Is he somehow communicating to me something that seems to mean something to him?" If these questions cannot be answered affirmatively, the person would do well to ask the Lord what has gone wrong. "Is there something you want to say to me that I don't want to hear? Or is there something I don't want to tell you?" By paying attention to the quality of the dialogue the person can learn to become more and more deeply transparent with God. The procedure could not be simpler. When we are expressing attitudes that are real and deep within us and relevant to our lives, prayer will be alive and engaging. When we are not, prayer will go dead. The director who has become accustomed to the fact that very often difficulties in prayer are due to the suppression of important attitudes and feelings does not quickly encourage directees to accept at face value statements like: "I had no time for prayer," or "I prayed only on the run." He tends to ask what was happening the last time the prayer was alive.

Many Christians feel that good prayer is always undisturbed and undisturbing. For them, peace is the principal criterion for deciding that their experience of God is authentic. This criterion is based on sound Christian experience; yet it can be misleading, for peace can have different meanings. It can mean a quiet sense of inner freedom that results from openness to God and willingness to respond to him. In this case it resembles the peace that Jesus left to his apostles at the Last Supper. It can also mean no more than the absence of strong feeling, particularly of fear, anger, disappointment, a sense of rejection, or guilt. If a person understands peace in this way and believes that such peace is a necessary sign of God's participation in his prayer, he may try to quell such feelings rather than pay attention to them. He may believe that they are intrusions leading him away from the condition that marks true prayer. His prayer, then, when he describes it only as "peaceful," may be a withdrawal from aspects of reality that upset him and could move him to action.

In light of the common belief that good prayer is always tranquil, a comment Ignatius makes in his instructions to retreat directors is striking. He tells them that the director should begin to ask questions of a retreatant if the retreatant's experience of prayer is persistently unruffled. When this happens, the director should inquire about the amount of time the retreatant is giving to prayer, about the circumstances and time of day when he prays, and about the other details of his routine. Ignatius is not alarmed at the prospect of sadness or upset; it is unruffled self-possession that bothers him.[5]

Often when we discuss with a person the history of his prayer for the previous few months, we get an intimation of what concerned Ignatius. People seem to be able to pray for weeks or months without experiencing any feeling that either encourages or disturbs them. There are no jagged peaks or deep valleys. There may not even be gentle rises or slight dips in the terrain. There is only "peace." It is hard to believe that a person engaged with the stresses and numerous decisions that daily life imposes can continue over a long period of time to experience such unruffled tranquility if he lets his whole self and all his significant experiences come into prayer. If he does not let them come into prayer, at some point he has to ask himself why he abstracts from significant experience when he prays. There is no question here of problem-solving. We are not suggesting that a person spend his time in prayer drawing up the family budget or rehearsing a coming interview with his boss. We are suggesting that, if a person's prayer prescinds from the affective attitudes that characterize his daily life, it is important that he know why that is happening. Is not Jesus speaking of these attitudes when he talks to us in the gospels? Are we prescinding from them because we are not at peace with them and half-consciously expect that they will bring about a sense of conflict if we admit them to prayer? Can prayer become a dialogue in which we let God meet those attitudes and so move closer to Christian integration?

When a person is making choices in his life—and these choices may be fairly ordinary day-to-day choices, for example, the attitude a person may take toward an administrator who has been harsh with him or a colleague who has maligned him—his feelings will come spontaneously into these choices and will emerge whenever he tries to present alternatives to the Lord. It is natural that this should be so. Choices in matters like these have much more to do with affective attitudes than with abstract questions of right and wrong. It is the colleague who makes me see red who is a challenge to Christian growth, not the person toward whom I feel bland and calm. The choice to take on another person's burden can be made without reluctance only if the burden is insignificant. The Christian choice is more likely to involve strong feelings of reluctance, even of rebellion, before the choice is finally made. The important choices we make take place in a prayer that is marked by turbulence until resolution comes. If our guiding principle is avoidance of all turbulence in prayer, then we may never have the opportunity to make such choices. Being able to tell the difference between the impulse that is from God and ultimately harmful impulses can only be developed in an atmosphere of prayer that contains at least some turbulence. Turbulence, then, is not a sign that a person's feelings are not being touched by God. Rather, it may well be a sign that he is facing the realities of his situation, including the reality of his response or lack of response.

If we are to expect turbulence on the way to recognition of the Lord's leading, however, how are we to know when the turbulence is the Lord's work and when it arises, for example, from our own laziness, fears, or sense of worthlessness? Again the dynamic of the relationship itself can be a help to us. The person can ask himself, "Am I expressing these important feelings to God?" If he is not, he can ask himself what is preventing him from doing so. Many of the feelings that deter us from making a choice that will open us to healing by the Lord, or promote companionship with Jesus will not bear the light of a question addressed to God. They flourish in us only insofar as we isolate ourselves by not expressing these feelings to him. When we are able to say to the Lord what we do feel, these feelings have a tendency to cease to distract us.

It is important to recognize that the impulses that do us harm when we are trying to respond to the Lord and be with him in his work for the world are often not focussed on evil. They simply stop us, prevent us from dialogue with the Lord or from doing the good we would like to do. A person who is moving steadily toward a freer acceptance of Jesus as human being as well as God may, for instance, find himself frequently distracted from dialogue with him by questions such as: "Who am I to expect him to speak to me in prayer?" or "Isn't it, after all, the teaching of the Church that can put us on safe ground in our lives, not what happens in prayer?" These are not trivial questions. The only perceptible effect of pondering them in prayer may, however, be the suspension of dialogue with the Lord.

When a person asks himself what most frequently prevents him from doing good, he may find that it is not impulses to evil, but a fear that he will be thought of as different by his friends and colleagues. Or it may be a question that cannot be answered like: "How do I know that spending energy being kind to people around me is really worthwhile?" Often the same question that now prevents a person from making creative Christian decisions also immobilized him ten years earlier. Inner arguments that persistently succeed in preventing us from responding to God are exceptionally hardy. The same question, if it is effective at all, can continue to be effective for decades. Such questions and inner arguments can be recognized for what they are by the fact that they seldom lead to answers and consistently stop movement toward the Lord.

Another set of criteria for deciding on the authenticity of one's religious experience is given in the tradition that derives from Paul's statement in Galatians: "But the fruit of the Spirit is love, joy, peace, patience, kindness, goodness, faithfulness, gentleness, self-control; against these there is no law."[6] These criteria, however, are not easily measured. Each of them can be mistaken for other reactions that do not indicate the action of the Spirit, and may even be contrary to that action. Relief at having made a decision can look like the peace of the Spirit, for example.[7] Witless enthusiasm can look like joy. Apathy sometimes resembles patience. Faced with such experience, the director is driven back to the question: How can we ever know?

The practical importance of the question is clear. Without objective criteria the director runs the risk of encouraging attitudes that may be attractive to him personally, but will ultimately impede the growth of the directee. How does one judge the spiritual value of humble dependence on the director, for instance? Some of the traditional statements on humility and obedience encourage us to think that such dependence is a sign of spiritual growth. Yet our experience often makes it clear that, in the light of the later history of the directee, what looked like development in humility and obedience was often an abdication of personal responsibility that, for the sake of growth, eventually had to be undone. What looks like growth in patience can be the result of a violent suppression of anger that will later show itself obliquely in frustration, depression, and the sense, in prayer, that the person faces an iron wall. If the person is ever to love, the suppression will have to be dissolved and the anger faced.

Perhaps this last example brings us closer to usable criteria. The Pauline signs as they are listed appear to be absolute and perfected. They do not appear so in experience. Rather, there is a process of development and sometimes unsteady growth in the virtues. But when their origin is the action of the Spirit, they come about not singly, but together. Patience does not make its appearance long after love and joy. It appears, in at least incipient form, along with them. The growth may be unequal—gentleness may for months be more obvious than joy—but it will never impede the growth of joy. The "fruits" appear as a unified growth, not a clutch of conflicting elements. And where there is conflict between the elements, or where one is totally lacking, the director must suspect illusion. For example, compulsive efforts at self-control usually lead to rigidity, lack of spontaneity and joy, and loss of peace. Such self-control may safely be judged illusory.

The quality of these criteria should be emphasized. They are positive fruits. They lead to an enduring sense of basic well-being. Fundamental joy, peace, consolation are the best criteria for evaluating one's prayer.[8]

In the last analysis, the director's ability to make use of these criteria in a concrete situation depends on his intuitive grasp of the criteria themselves and his intuitive recognition of their developing presence in the other person. If the director does not know from experience, for example, that peace is more than relief from tension, he will not find it a helpful criterion when it appears in the directee. If he does not have at least the beginning of an intuitive understanding of patience, he may find himself looking for bouncy joy in a person whose genuine response to the Spirit at the time is patient endurance of depression.

Breadth of outlook and empathy develop as the director personally experiences his own development and his own use of these criteria, and as he sees increasing numbers of people who show these signs of being moved by the Spirit in an unexpected variety of ways. His own categories begin to broaden, differentiate, and become more flexible as he listens to others' experiences of God and lets himself perceive newness and originality.

We all have our favorite images and examples of the spiritual life. A director may personally prefer a dedicated, competent administrator like Dag Hammarskjöld or St. Pius X to a charismatic, lyric figure like Francis of Assisi. Such a preference need not affect the quality of his direction. But if he sees every Francis who comes to him as spiritually immature, then he—and his directees—will be in trouble.

There is another criterion that appears after the early stages of explicit spiritual growth: the developing sense of the reality of God as someone who is not within the directee's control. This criterion, too, is interior; it shows itself in the surprise and even anxiety that a directee experiences in prayer when the Lord appears in a new way; for instance, when a directee experiences God as still looking at him with love after he has lied to keep from losing face—a new experience, and one that frightens as well as consoles.

This experience of the reality and uncontrollability of the Other reaches its peak in the experience of Jesus as a person who cares for others and for the world. Every Christian shares

in that reality to some extent, some consciously, most unconsciously.[9] This experience of Jesus shows itself in an ability
to live by one's own convictions despite other people's op-
position to those convictions; in a breadth of empathy that
transcends social and economic class; in a deepening trust of
the Father of reality; in a willingness to engage in the war
against evil and to stand for justice and mercy even when one
must die small deaths in defense of them; and a willingness
to die those deaths and leave resurrection to the Father.

Again, an example from Thomas Merton can illustrate what
is meant. He is on his way to the Abbey of Gethsemani in the
hope of entering:

> It was a strange thing. Mile after mile my desire to be in the
> monastery increased beyond belief. I was altogether absorbed in
> that one idea. And yet, paradoxically, mile after mile my indif-
> ference increased, and my interior peace. What if they did not
> receive me? Then I would go to the army. But surely that would
> be a disaster? Not at all. If, after all this, I was rejected by the
> monastery and had to be drafted, it would be quite clear that it
> was God's will. I had done everything that was in my power; the
> rest was in His hands. And for all the tremendous and increasing
> intensity of my desire to be in the cloister, the thought that I
> might find myself, instead, in an army camp no longer troubled
> me in the least.
>
> I was free, I had recovered my liberty. I belonged to God, not
> to myself: and to belong to Him is to be free, free of all the
> anxieties and worries and sorrows that belong to this earth, and
> the love of the things that are in it.[10]

Merton is describing a paradoxical state. His desire is intense,
but he is willing to accept without demurring the frustration
of that desire. Now that he has made his own decision, he
leaves the future to a God in whose love he has confidence.

The reference to the experience of God and of Jesus leads us
to a final criterion which Christian tradition has seen as one
of the paramount tests by which people are able to decide

whether it is God who is leading them in a particular situation. It can be summarized with the question, "Is it like God?" or "Is it like what Jesus would do?" We can readily find that the point of these questions gets blunted by hermeneutical consideration or by adherence to a purely external model. However, if the questions are used appropriately they can be of crucial help in determining what is of God. An example of appropriate use of these questions is found in *The life of Martin*,[11] a fourth-century work of hagiography. Martin has a vision and has to decide whether the vision is really from the Lord. He decides that it is not because the figure of Jesus in the vision is dressed in the raiment of a Roman imperator. Martin's conclusion is, "I will believe that Christ has come only when I see him wearing the garments of the Passion."

Martin's question, "Is it like the Lord?" is one that we, too, can use. If we are being led in a direction that, however much good it may yield, will also bring about results that are harmful, even destructive of persons, then we have good reason to conclude that this direction is not like those that the Lord takes.

The Fathers of the Church describe Christians as imitators of God. They would bear other people's burdens and not use any power and wealth they might have to make other people serve them—not because such behavior conflicts with rational morality, but because it is not the way God acts.

But the usefulness of this criterion depends on how well I have come to know God. If I do not see him as someone who cares about what happens to his world, then I will not recognize his concern in impulses that move me to prefer other people's good to my own. I will run a risk of overlooking impulses that are concerned not with my own good, but with the good, for example, of poor people I have never seen, people who may need something that I can give, though only with considerable sacrifice on my part.

Central to Ignatius's ability to "tell the difference" was the fact that he wanted to do great things for God. He was not interested simply in living his life reasonably well. So he tried to find out what great things God might want done. He thus came to look at the life of Jesus, and there he found the beginnings of the answer to his question. Because God cared about his world, he sent his Son; because the Son cared about God's world, he was willing to commit himself to live for that world even though it meant deprivation for himself. By contemplating Jesus, Ignatius came to desire to adopt the mind and heart and values of Jesus and to live as he lived. As he grew in the knowledge and love of Jesus, he became more and more able to tell the difference between impulses that were from the Lord and those that were not.[12]

What exactly does one use criteria for? Do they describe the state a person should be in, the ideals he should be held to? If criteria are seen in this way, the director can easily substitute his own estimate of the person's growth for the Spirit's action, and so exhort him into blind alleys. At the very least, he will substitute abstractions for reality in his way of seeing the progress of the direction. The value of criteria for the director seems to be simply this: they give him ways of determining whether the direction is toward the Lord and his people or up the garden path and of helping the directee make a similar judgment. The director is always a secondary person in the dialogue between the Lord and the directee. It is not he who calls the shots. But he has the responsibility to decide for himself and to help the directee decide whether the process of direction is leading to good or harm. The directee wants help to avoid illusion. As a director grows, he will learn to fulfill this responsibility without interfering with the action of the Spirit or the response of the directee.

Because spiritual growth is basically interior, the criteria for observing it are necessarily interior. However, if there is an interior life which in no way shows itself in external action or reaction, it will have little interest for most directors. Precisely because the inner criteria are so plastic, and because an authentic relationship with God moves toward a unity of external and internal life, some external indications are necessary.

If these external indices are kept in their appropriately secondary place, they can be very helpful as checks on the use of the inner criteria. The whole Christian spiritual tradition, for instance, is sturdily suspicious of the authenticity of mystical prayer when the mystic can never take time to help wash the dishes. Some indication of how the person interacts with others, how he actually responds—not simply thinks he responds—to his community or family can be immensely helpful as a check on the validity of the director's and his own view of his inner life.

The Christian tradition is also suspicious of the authenticity of mystical prayer when the mystic refuses to listen to any voice other than his own inner one.[13] Authentic religious experiences move toward a unity of individual and community and lead to openness to other voices, especially to openness to the voice of legitimate authority in the church. Such openness may lead to tension and struggle since authentic obedience must faithfully listen to both inner and outer voices and cannot too quickly accept one over the other. An unwillingness to listen to the voice of others—and especially to the voice of legitimate authority—is a sign that at some point the person's prayer has stopped making him free.

By and large, there will be reciprocal interaction between inner life and external reality—and porous terms these have to be, for they are as identical as they are distinct. Experience of spiritual direction always makes us more aware that growth in a person's inner response to the Lord of reality normally shows itself in his external life—his relationships, the texture and direction of his work, the life choices he makes. When there is no outward Christian development, it will be seen sooner or later that there is something askew in his inner development.

At the same time, we cannot view external criteria as primary since both the action of the Spirit and human motivation are so varied, work on so many different levels, and are so basically interior that external action by itself is almost useless as a criterion. "You will know them by their fruits,"[14] but the external fruits of the Spirit will usually be indiscernible to the director unless he has some sense of the person's inner growth. The lay person who does not attend church services every Sunday and the pastor who leaves some of his parish duties undone may actually be more alive before the Lord than the person who is doing everything "right." If the director makes external criteria primary, he may be discouraging inner growth by providing a schema of external standards that the directee feels he has to meet and that he feels represent the only response to God he will be called upon to make. "But I did everything they told me to do" is a very dispiriting comment on any spiritual direction in which the speaker may have participated.

Then, too, we have to expect that the action of the Spirit will often be surprising and will override the personal presuppositions of the director. Indeed, if the directee is living in a genuinely lively relationship with the Lord, one indication of this is the fact that his actions will sometimes surprise, and even disconcert, the director. If the director's criteria tend to be external, he may discount the importance of such originality and thus tend to stifle the Spirit.

It always has to be remembered that all these criteria are, in experience, not so much states as processes, and that when the inner life is really alive, they will be expressions of growth—fluctuating, undulating, now leaping, now quiet. Change will not be a negative sign, nor will anxiety or resistance. The key positive sign will be the growing fullness and ripening texture of the person's life as it grows toward the maturity of Christ. Mistakes will be made, blind alleys tried, but with this positive sign as criterion one can find one's way and can be relatively sure that whatever illusions still reside in one's images of God, self, and world will also have a chance to be corrected by contact with the Lord and with life.

Perhaps the basic theological reason for the growing popularity of teams of directors, who while working as individuals with directees discuss their practice with one another, is that in such exchanges—in other words, in such informal, ad hoc communities—the breadth of action of the Spirit is more likely to be recognized than it would be by an individual director working alone. The Spirit is communitarian. He seems to breach directors' individual limitations and broaden their vision more readily in such groups.

PART THREE

Aspects of the Relationship Between Director and Directee

Becoming a Spiritual Director

It seems evident that a spiritual direction that takes the facilitation of the personal encounter with God as its proper sphere is working with the central—not a peripheral—movement of the Christian life. By what right does one do this work? There is no office or order of spiritual director in the Church. Some of the most outstanding spiritual directors in Christian history—like Catherine of Siena and Ignatius of Loyola—either never had an office or orders, or did much of their work of direction before they held such an office. Generally speaking, effective spiritual directors are discovered by the Christian community; they do not put themselves forward without first having others seek their help. Because priests and ministers stand out publicly in the churches as spiritual leaders, most often it is they who have been sought out as spiritual directors. But ordination is not necessary (nor, as we shall see, sufficient) for effective spiritual direction. What, then, is the relationship of the spiritual director to the Church as covenant community?

We can see more clearly what spiritual direction has to do with that community if we look more closely at what happens in spiritual direction. Whatever else he does or receives, the directee at least communicates with another member of the Church something of his relationship with God. He does not hold his inner life in isolation from the people of God. He confides it to them in the person of the spiritual director. What directors most basically bring to the relationship with directees is their membership in the Christian community and their sharing in the faith of that community. Whether or not they have special charisms, knowledge, and talents, they provide an opportunity for a directee to look at his relationship with the Lord and thread a path through his illusions with the help of a fellow member of the community. Even if they say nothing, the fact that they listen enables the directee to share his experience with the community and not close that experience in upon itself, where for want of air it could become crabbed and deluded.

The more conscious directors are of the life of the Christian community and the more knowledgeable they are about the experienced relationship of that community with the Lord and with all reality, the more helpful they are likely to be to directees. But their authority arises basically from the fact that they share in the faith-life of the Christian community as it experiences its dialogue with the Lord. This makes the director first of all a brother or a sister of the directee and provides the basic ingredient for the informal, nonhierarchic—"just two people talking"—but creative atmosphere that seems to characterize helpful direction today.

Thus, the primary basis for the trust placed in a spiritual director is the director's membership in the faith community. The directee puts his trust in a brother or a sister to help him to grow in his relationship with the Lord. Before we proceed, we want to underline that basis. Trust can be founded on many bases; for example, one can trust another because he has an office in the church, or because he is tall and has a commanding presence, or because he has been experienced as trustworthy by others whom one respects. If, however, the trust does not ultimately become rooted in one's own experience of the director as trustworthy, then the relationship will never become the brotherly or sisterly relationship which seems to characterize the most helpful direction today.

It is obvious that not every Christian deserves the kind of trust spiritual direction seems to require. It may be less obvious that not all ordained ministers deserve such trust. For example, a recent study of the Roman Catholic priesthood reported that a large majority could be described in this fashion:

> The chief area in which underdeveloped priests manifest their lack of psychological growth is in their relationships with other persons. These relationships are ordinarily distant, highly stylized, and frequently unrewarding for the priest and for the other person . . . they have few close friends . . . In underdeveloped priests there are evidences of passivity, exaggerated docility, and a tendency to identify themselves through the role of the priesthood rather than through their own personalities. . . . They mistrust themselves, feel unworthy, and frequently hold back from using their full capacities. . . . It is surprising to find in this group of men a general inability to articulate a deep level of personal religious faith. [1]

It is clear that such men would have grave difficulties attempting to be the kind of spiritual director envisaged in this book. These men have their greatest difficulties precisely in the area of relationships. They would not inspire trust in relatively mature people who were seeking spiritual direction. From the description it would appear that these men also do not have much appropriated experience of a loving God and so could hardly mediate such a God to directees. Comparable data are not available for other groups from which spiritual directors are drawn. Both men and women who share the same characteristics as these underdeveloped priests should be discouraged from the work of spiritual direction until they have overcome the developmental lags from which they suffer, since the basis for trust in such persons cannot be their experienced trustworthiness as brothers or sisters growing in their relationships with God and others.

The kinds of men and women most likely to engender trust in others are those described in the same study as developed persons. They are not perfect, but they are relatively mature. They show signs of having engaged in life and with people.

They are optimistic, but not naive, good-humored, but not glad-handers. They have suffered, but not been overcome by suffering. They have loved and been loved and know the struggle of trying to be a friend to another. They have friends for whom they care deeply. They have experienced failure and sinfulness—their own and others'—but seem at ease with themselves in a way that indicates an experience of being saved and freed by a power greater than the power of failure and sin. They are relatively unafraid of life with all its light and darkness, all its mystery.

Spiritual directors will also need a deep faith in the desire and ability of God to communicate with his people, not only as a community, but as individuals too. This faith, if it is to be firm enough to sustain them in their work, must spring from their own experience of God. Such experience-based faith will be the ground for their working assumption that there is no one with whom God does not desire to communicate. Spiritual directors have experienced God as communicating with them in all *their* reality, and this experience grounds their assumption about all other people.

This experience-based conviction leads to a contemplative attitude in directors that is open and eager to discover God's ways with all kinds of people. Their own experience of God's saving love and challenging presence makes them wonderers—wondering how God has communicated with and is communicating with other people. Aware that their own experience of God is limited, they want to know more about him and expect to learn more about him by listening to other people's experience of him. Such an attitude of faith in God and in his presence to others can engender trust.

The contemplative attitude which directors have developed through their own prayer and their own experience of being directed also enables them to be more open and less resistive to newness and surprise. It enables them, in other words, to listen to the experience of others and to learn from them. Directees get the impression that such directors want to hear about their real experiences in prayer (not the "right" ones or the "expected" ones) and so become willing, and gradually able, to talk about them. Even so, it can take a long time, sometimes years, for a person to confide the experiences of God that affect him most deeply.

The contemplative attitude also leads directors to believe that the light will overcome the darkness in others. They have experienced their own fears and darkness, their own demons, and have also experienced salvation from them. They have experienced God as the one who loves first[2]—the one who loved them when they were dead in their sins[3]—who loves them with all their ambivalence, all their love and hatred, all their lusts, their fears, their selfishness and unselfishness. They have been enabled by such experiences of God to love themselves and to change. Thus, they have an attitude of quiet trust that God will do similar things for others. In other words, they have become less afraid of real people and of the darker sides of real people because they have experienced a God who loves and saves real people like themselves, warts and moles and all.

This attitude is not a Pollyannaish, bland optimism about people. Those who have experienced themselves as loved sinners have experienced themselves precisely as sinners. They have, perhaps, been almost overwhelmed by the experience of their own evil tendencies and the strength of their fears. They do not blind themselves to such tendencies and fears in themselves or in others. But they have experienced that such darkness could not overcome the light,[4] that "where sin increased, grace abounded all the more."[5] "They know where all the bodies are buried," but the knowledge has not destroyed their hope.

It needs to be emphasized that directees are real people, and as such they are just as varied, just as ambivalent, just as attractive and unattractive as are, for example, directors themselves. Real people can be scintillating, and they can be boring, often within the same hour. They can be banal and they can be inspired. They can be concerned about momentous and serious issues, and about trivia. They can be sunny, and they can be gloomy. In their prayer life they will show all these dispositions and more. Spiritual directors who want to foster a relationship between such people and their God need to have "a surplus of warmth."[6]

A spiritual director needs to take stock honestly. Do I really love a variety of people, warts and moles and all? Do I find myself enjoying people, and am I able to laugh at and live with their foibles? Am I interested in listening to their cares and concerns? The words of Cesar Chavez to college volunteers who could not understand why the farm workers were solidly behind the American involvement in the Vietnam War might also be applied to spiritual directors: "I told them to understand that farm workers are human beings. 'If you don't understand that, you are going to be mighty disappointed. You have to understand that you may work very hard, and the day will come when they will just boot you out, or they don't appreciate what you are doing.' And I warned them not to have any hidden agenda."[7]

How does this "surplus of warmth," this love for people as they are, show itself in spiritual direction? It appears in three attitudes: commitment, effort to understand, and spontaneity.[8] Commitment is the spiritual director's willingness to help the directee grow in union with God and to commit his time, his resources, and himself to that end. Effort to understand means that the spiritual director tries to maintain a contemplative attitude to the directee, tries to perceive how he is experiencing the Lord and life. Spontaneity means that the spiritual director is himself not controlled and inhibited by his role as spiritual director, but is able to express his own feelings, thoughts, and hopes when expressing them will be helpful to the directee. Without spontaneity, "commitment and effort to understand" will appear cold, impersonal, and stereotyped."[9]

Why is such warmth needed in spiritual directors? In the first place, spiritual direction can mean hard, often unrewarding work. Directors enter into deep relationships with many people, and their own hearts are laid bare over and over again. At such close range their own failings are magnified, and they expose themselves to having them flung back in their faces in moments of anger. If they succeed in helping others to be free before God and before life, they run the risk of being blamed, sometimes by people in authority, for the consequences—especially the early consequences—of the new freedom their directees have found. If they do not succeed in helping, they run the risk of being considered bunglers.

Secondly, directees have to experience such commitment, effort to understand, and honest and spontaneous humanness in order to risk entrusting themselves to spiritual directors. People do not wear their hearts on their sleeves. When they seek the help of a spiritual director, they do not know with certainty whether anyone can help or cares to help; one woman cried with relief when she found out that a spiritual director would help her with her prayer. Many do not know whether their thoughts, their feelings, their experiences are worth another person's time or are intelligible. They are afraid of being thought crazy or laughable. Or they are afraid that what they have to say may seem "so ordinary," "so banal," "so common." They need to sense the warmth of the director in order to even begin the process.

This kind of warmth shows itself in patient listening, perhaps, more than in any other way. We are back again to the contemplative attitude. Life does not seem to provide many opportunities to talk to someone who really listens and tries to understand. All of us seem to have too much on our minds to pay close attention to most other people. But spiritual directors make it their profession precisely to be listeners, to try to put aside their own cares, their own prejudices, their own desires for a place in the conversational sun in order to see the world through the eyes of this other person, to understand what he feels and experiences, and not judge.

There are no books that teach one how to be warm, no training programs that develop warmth. To be able to do this kind of listening spiritual directors must first of all be warm, interested people. What Braatøy says of the psychoanalyst applies directly to the spiritual director:

> . . . the psychoanalyst can be compared with an instrument. This instrument must have some capacities. . . . If a knife is made of iron it cannot perform the tasks one expects of a steel knife. For similar reasons, one cannot *demand* "surplus of warmth" from a therapist. It must belong more or less to his inherent capacities.[10]

He then says that psychoanalytic institutes must do all they can to screen out candidates for training who do not possess this quality. We make the same suggestion to those who must screen potential spiritual directors. They must make sure that the potential director loves people in an earthy, honest, felt way.

Spiritual directors require self-confidence. Without it they tend to need constant reassurance that they are doing the right thing. They are continually anxious lest they make a mistake. They need too many tangible signs of success and find the internal criteria of discernment difficult to use with assurance. They are hard put to bear with the sometimes long and painful process of growth that people go through while receiving spiritual direction. They also tend to go by the book and can, thus, prevent directees from proceeding at their own pace. They do not inspire confidence in mature directees.

The last paragraph should not be taken to mean that self-confident spiritual directors are not frightened at times, even frequently. Spiritual directors with a good deal of personal experience of prayer know that they are entering on holy ground and they do so with at least some fear and trembling. It is right that they be in awe and afraid that they might falter and fail the directee. Such feelings are, however, realistic and appropriate and do not incapacitate them. Indeed, directors who do not demonstrate such an attitude (what one might call humility) along with their self-confidence will seem brash to mature directees and will not gain their trust. The lack of confidence we mean is a debilitating feeling which stems, not from awe before the living God, but from self-concern, self-doubt, and fear of life. Those who fear life cannot foster in others an open relationship with the living God.

Even granted an initial warmth, listening in the way described above is not easy. For one thing, spiritual directors can be caught in a situation of conflicting interests. Often enough, they are unaware of how the conflict affects their listening. They may, for instance, see themselves as acting in the interest of those who come for their help and yet feel some responsibility to protect a third person or an institution. For example, a spiritual director may find out that a directee, a divinity student about to be ordained, is a kleptomaniac. The director may become irate and begin to think of ways to keep this man from getting ordained, and thus be unable to listen to him and find out why he is now mentioning his difficulty.

Moreover, spiritual directors, like everyone else, are all so enmeshed in and part of the cultural, social, political, and religious mores and institutions of society and various sub-societies that they are unconsciously their agents and, so, prone to want to protect them from threat or aberration. The totally unbiased spiritual director is a chimaera, of course. However, directors can try to protect their directees from their biases through personal spiritual direction, wide reading and experience, openness to diverse viewpoints, and competent supervision.

Spiritual directors also can listen better to their directees if they do not depend on them for personal satisfaction and security. Thus, for example, they need friends who are not directees so that "success" with directees is not necessary for their self-respect. Otherwise they may need their directees too much and so be unable to listen to all that they communicate and to challenge them when necessary. Moreover, they need enough friends and other sources of self-respect to retain personal equanimity without nervously needing the approval of people in authority over or close to their directees. For they may not receive such approval when the directees do not conform to what these people expect. The ability to listen with warmth to people who are growing in freedom before the Lord requires in directors an inner freedom from fear of what authorities or other persons in the church, or in the family, for example, will think.

Finally, in order to listen in this way directors must be relatively unafraid of strong emotions, deep feelings, mysterious experiences, and all that is human. If a director cannot tolerate strong anger in himself or others, he will be unable to listen to it in directees. Soon he will not be hearing about angry feelings in prayer, not because they do not occur, but because directees will recognize consciously or semiconsciously that such feelings are taboo in his presence. The danger is that they might translate such taboos to their relationship with the Lord and so express themselves selectively to him.

Directors must also be relatively tolerant of painful experiences in themselves and others. An authentic love for their directees will show itself in a willingness to be with them as they suffer the pains of growth and not try to take the pain away. If they can do this, they will be more able to listen and will communicate their willingness to hear such pain.

These attitudes are not achievements to be arrived at by dint of hard work and diligent attention to responsibilities. Rather, they are gifts to be prayed for and to be grateful for. Moreover, they are not fixed and absolute realities that one must have, but ideals realistically to be hoped for. No spiritual director will ever be able to live up to all these ideals all the time, perhaps not much more than half the time. Spiritual directors can be depressed or angry or sick or worried, and be unable to listen as alertly and warmly as they would like. If their basic attitudes are warmth and trust in the Lord and in his ability and desire to communicate, then they will be able to live with their own frailties, ask help of the Lord who is desirous of their good, and count on the humanity and sympathy of their directees to forgive the lapses and remember the underlying warmth.

While warmth is not a trait that can be learned in a training program, it does not follow that spiritual directors are born, not made. It is evident from our description of the person of the director that we believe potential directors should be men and women of relatively wide experience of life. The broader the base, the less constricted and constricting they will be as persons. Experiences of living in varied socioeconomic and cultural groups tend to make the director's own expectations more flexible and differentiated and thus more open to new and varied experiences in others. We have already spoken of the need for directors to be men and women who themselves have experienced and are experiencing a growing and deepening relationship with the Lord. Spiritual directors need not be engaged in advanced stages of mystical prayer, but they should have experienced themselves as sinners loved by God. We believe that they should also have experienced the challenge of meeting the Lord Jesus not just as personal savior, but also as one who calls us to decision and self-sacrifice. A director who has experienced only the comfort of salvation would have difficulty understanding and helping someone who is experiencing the more subtle movements of the spirit that occur when the relationship begins to change toward more and more identification with Jesus on his mission. At least this much experience of the deepening relationship with Jesus is a prerequisite for engaging in long-term spiritual direction.

Besides personal experience, spiritual directors need study as part of their continuing becoming. They do not need doctorates in spirituality to be competent, but they do need to have more knowledge than personal experience and common sense alone can supply. In what follows we set forth for discussion areas where we believe study is necessary.

Spiritual directors universally recommend the Bible as a source of personal prayer. We believe that the best way (not the only way) to use Scripture for prayer is to take it as much as possible on its own terms, that is, understanding the various books and passages as they were originally intended to be understood. Thus, spiritual directors ought to have enough understanding of modern scriptural studies to be able to help directees hear the word of God in a relatively informed way.

Spiritual directors need an informed and intelligent understanding of the faith of the Church in order to help people to freedom before the Lord. Many people are imprisoned in inadequate and childish conceptions of who God is and what he wants. All of us, moreover, are conditioned by the philosophical presuppositions that have undergirded the theology and catechesis of the churches since at least the medieval and Reformation periods. It is not easy with either set of expectations to let God be the ever greater One he is, greater than all our perceptions and assumptions. Throughout this book we have maintained that spiritual directors as such are not teachers. However, a mature and intelligent grasp of modern theology will help spiritual directors put things in such a way that their directees are more able to let the *real* God relate to them.

A simple example: Many of us grew up with a somewhat schizoid view of prayer. On the one hand, we were exhorted to (and given multiple examples of) petitionary prayer. We let God know our needs and asked him to intervene. On the other hand, we were also taught that God was all-knowing and unchangeable, both attributes that make the value of petitionary prayer at least questionable. Most people solved the dilemma in practice by forgetting the latter teaching. But the theory of God we were taught has had an effect on some people's prayer and even led them to give up petitionary and other dialogical prayer. A spiritual director who understands that philosophical presuppositions grounded the theory of God and that these philosophical presuppositions are not revealed nor necessarily true as they were stated might be able to help a directee try a type of prayer that expects God to react and be concerned. The director need not go into a theological disquisition on the subject; his knowledge of theology will give him the confidence to suggest the approach and to handle any objection without becoming defensive.

Spiritual directors do not need to be specialists in theology or knowledgeable in all its areas. But they do need a solid grounding in theology, at least enough to know how conditioned by culture and philosophical assumptions dogmatic formulations are.

Finally, spiritual directors ought to have some knowledge of the history of spirituality, enough to know that God has dealt with people in various ways and to understand the interaction among personality, culture, and the action of God in the development of a personal spiritual life and of schools of spirituality. Some knowledge of the diversity of Christian religious experience and a sympathetic awareness of non-Christian religious experience can help directors transcend their personal absolutes and open them to a greater sense of wonder toward the manifold experience of people with God. Knowledge that is won through study can help directors come to the healthy confidence and breadth they need.

To theological knowledge we must also add, today, some knowledge of modern psychology. "Whoever, therefore, wants to help others spiritually must not only be himself a spiritual person and have a command of spiritual experience, but also have sufficient psychological knowledge (without, however, falling into the error of wanting to do psychotherapy and thereby succumbing to the delusion that his psychological knowledge is sufficient for that)."[11]

Spiritual directors and potential spiritual directors may be shaking their heads in wonderment at this list of prerequisites. But recall what we said earlier about the centrality of spiritual direction to the pastoral ministry of the Church. The Church has always sought to prepare people as professionally as possible for its ministry. Spiritual direction should be no exception to this practice. Presentation of the ideal of such preparation should not, however, be taken to mean that spiritual direction of high quality has not taken place and cannot take place without such preparation. We have already mentioned the cases of Catherine of Siena and Ignatius of Loyola. In ordinary cases, however, professional preparation should not be too easily dispensed with.

Becoming a spiritual director is a lifelong process. Theology and personal experience point to an ever greater God, and so spiritual directors can expect to be continually called to further growth. Their experience of other people in relationship with God will challenge them to prayer, deeper reflection, a fresh look at what they have studied, and further study. The adventure has no end in this life.

The Basis for the Relationship Between Director and Directee

If spiritual direction is understood basically as the imparting of directions for right living and right praying, then the person of the director and the depth of his faith and his prayer life are clearly not as important as what he knows and what authority he has. However, in the understanding of spiritual direction that we propose, it is clear that the person of the director is central. He or she must be in a conscious relationship with God and also be able to relate well with people. To facilitate the development of another's relationship with God, the spiritual director (and every ministering person) needs to be a sacramental sign of God's loving care. It is true that God can relate to people without the mediation of anyone else, and even in spite of poor mediation; his usual way is, however, through other people. So the quality of the Church's ministers must be a great concern; it is not simply their knowledge that is central, but their whole being. This is especially true of spiritual directors: their persons, their faith and hope and love, their capacity for relationships become crucial for the work they do.

Our focus on the qualities of directors and on the relationship between director and directee will require comparisons with and borrowings from the work of psychiatrists and psychologists who have, in this century, taught us so much about the characteristics of helping relationships. Some may feel that the recourse to psychiatry and psychology is unwarranted on the grounds that spiritual direction is a supernatural ministry. It should by now be obvious that we do not share this viewpoint. For us, the relationship between God and a human person cannot be parcelled out into natural and supernatural elements, nor can the relationship between director and directee. These relationships involve all that is human, and so we need to learn from those disciplines and those investigators who have, with much personal courage and humility, reflected upon and subjected to the scrutiny of others their helping relationships.

It also needs to be said that with the emergence of modern theories of therapy and counseling pastoral care has too often looked like a carbon copy of these secular models. Much pastoral counseling, especially, has seemed to many to be little more than secular counseling done by a minister. A case can be made for such practice, we realize. The incarnation means that all that is in the human can be divinized. At the same time, ministering people need to be aware of the specifically religious resources of the Christian tradition which can be brought to bear to help people lead richer and fuller lives. While we borrow, with gratitude, concepts and practice from the psychological fields, we believe that spiritual direction is a helping relationship distinct from psychotherapy and psychological counseling. It has its own contribution to make to the effort of helping people live more meaningfully and fully in our world.

Spiritual direction proposes to help people relate personally to God, to let God relate personally to them, and to enable them to live the consequences of that relationship. The development of any interpersonal relationship is a mysterious process; hence, anyone who agrees to help two or more individuals develop their relationship should approach the task with humility and reverence, in the spirit of a companion rather than a trailblazer. How much more evident this is when one of the persons in the dialogue is Mystery itself! Spiritual direction is a helping relationship, but the help offered is more like that of a companion on a journey than of an expert who, before the journey begins, advises what roads to take and answers the traveler's questions. The companion tries to help the traveler read the maps, avoid dead ends, and watch out for potholes. The Mystery we call God is just that—mystery; not mystery in the sense of an unknown, but eventually knowable, stranger, but mystery in the sense that he is too rich, too deep, and too loving to be knowable and is, therefore, God. Spiritual directors can only be helping companions to those who travel the way of such a Lord.

Thus, the only authority they can have is the authority of their own persons as people who belong to that Lord and to his community and who seem to take seriously their own relationship to him and to his community. As such, they are asked for help by other members of the community.

As a consequence of the nature of spiritual direction, spiritual directors should eschew any mannerisms, modes of dress, office arrangements, or ways of speaking that indicate that they know the way, have the answers, or can guarantee "success" in prayer. The initial impressions directors give should reflect their convictions about the nature of direction. It can be all too tempting to give the impression that the directee's problems will be over and that he will surely find the Lord if only he will put himself into the director's hands.

At the same time, directors can go to the opposite extreme and become so folksy, so "brotherly" or "sisterly" that they give the impression that they have nothing to offer directees except camaraderie. The people of God who seek spiritual direction expect more help than this.

Thus, the initial impression given by office arrangements and manner of approach should be one of willingness to be a companion on the way and of seriousness (not devoid of humor and humanity) about being a companion. There are no clear cut prescriptions for conveying such an impression. Spiritual directors who see themselves basically as companions will convey the impression. Those who merely pay lip service to this conviction will never convey this impression.

In the last chapter we stated that spiritual directors need a "surplus of warmth" in order to be effective. When directors stress the negative or dark sides of directees' experience, they can seem condescending rather than genuinely warm. It seems easier to depict the foibles and follies of people than it is to emphasize their strengths, and more fun too. We have noticed that audiences sit straighter when speakers describe the unmasking of resistance and parade foibles, sins, and symptoms before them, whether the speakers are spiritual directors, moral theologians, psychiatrists, or psychologists. There seems to be a morbid satisfaction in discovering the shadows behind the smiling face, the "hidden" (and almost by definition unsavory) motivation behind the "facade." But spiritual directors generally find that directees are likable and have strength, courage, and desires that are admirable. They find, in other words, that warmth is elicited from them by what they see and hear from directees. Indeed, it might safely be stated that unless such an elicited warmth is engaged the direction will not prosper; that is, unless the director experiences warmth for this directee because of the directee's own qualities, then the direction will not become a relationship of peers who are working together. Such warmth may not be immediately given and can—and should—go hand in hand with a realistic view of the directee. But it does need to be present.

In spiritual direction, the major characteristic of directees that elicits such uncondescending warmth is their desire to develop a deeper relationship with the Lord. This desire meets the hope of the director that he can help foster such a relationship. The director, in fact, makes an alliance with that desire in the directee. Both parties recognize that the desire is there, and both agree that they will work together to attain that desire. The directee expects that the director will maintain his alliance with that desire in him even when he is strongly resisting it. The "working alliance"[1] in spiritual direction, in other words, is that aspect of the relationship between director and directee which enables the directee to continue to work toward the fulfillment of his purpose in seeking direction. On the part of the director, the working alliance is an expression of the warmth for this other person that has been elicited by his sincere desire to know the Lord better.

All help toward personal growth that is not manipulative or caretaking depends upon a working alliance. For example, in psychoanalysis the working alliance relies on the "reasonable ego";[2] in Rogerian counseling, on the tendency to self-actualization;[3] in Rankian therapy, on the will to health.[4] All of these concepts seem to refer to an essentially similar reality in people, that is, to the desire—in spite of their sometimes self-defeating, neurotic, and resistive behavior—to live more fully, with more honesty and health and less self-inflicted pain. This desire in people makes counseling and therapy possible. This desire keeps them at the task of overcoming their resistance to growth and change. In the same way, the desire for a deeper union with God keeps directees at the task of overcoming their resistance. The desire of a client, in fact, keeps him in a situation where resistance is bound to occur, namely in therapy, just as the desire of a directee keeps him in prayer and spiritual direction.

It must be a powerful desire that can go so persistently against the grain of entrenched and heavily defended personality patterns. What is its source? The comparison with spiritual direction makes it possible to detect a common source to both desires, whether it is recognized as such or not: the indwelling Spirit of the living God. In other words, the drive to more wholeness and integrity in those who seek therapy and counseling may ultimately have the same source as the desire for a deeper union with God in those who seek spiritual direction. The difference would lie in the reflective awareness of the nature of the source.

"Rumors of angels"[5] can appear in the most unlikely places. If we look at the experience people have and try to make sense of it, we begin to see the possibility that the desire for a fuller and more integrated life derives from the same source as the conscious desire to love God with all one's heart. It may not seem the same at first glance because it has not been appropriated by faith. There is no reason, however, to see the one as a "natural" desire, the other as "super-natural." There is no litmus paper of the inner life that allows us to make such distinctions. When and if an "a-religious" person who has sought therapy because he wanted a more integrated and less self-defeating life comes to believe in the mystery we call God, he may recognize that from his first impulse toward greater integration he has been impelled by the same Spirit who now clearly cries, "Abba, Father,"[6] but who even then was interceding for him with sighs too deep for words.[7]

These reflections bring us to the realization that spiritual directors consciously ally themselves with the indwelling Spirit and the expression of that Spirit in the desire of directees for "more" in the way of life and union with God. They make this alliance in order to help directees overcome those elements in themselves that war against the Spirit. They make it because they experience in directees the strength that comes from the Spirit, a strength that has remained alive in spite of all the fears and resistance, the weakness and the sin that are realities in them as they are in their directors.

The person and attitudes of the director which we discussed in the last chapter are the perceived grounds for the directee's willingness to enter into a working alliance with a particular director. The directee trusts that the director believes in a God who wants to communicate with him and also believes in the directee's Spirit-inspired capacity to respond in kind to God.

A working alliance depends very much on a mutual agreement between director and directee as to what the directee wants and what the director can do. Thus, it is important for spiritual direction that both parties agree on its purpose and its means. If that agreement is not clearly made, then any further work—but especially confrontation of resistances and handling of difficulties in the relationship—will be in jeopardy. One can expect that in any spiritual direction that lasts for some time the director and directee will at some point come to cross purposes. Without a strong working alliance based upon a mutual acceptance of what spiritual direction is, they will weather the storm only with great difficulty. Put concretely, with such a strong alliance a directee can continue to pray and to work hard in the sessions with the director even when angry words have been exchanged in the previous hour

In the fields of counseling and psychotherapy the issues we are now discussing come under the heading of "contract setting."[8] We prefer the less formal term "agreement" and note that this agreement can be in the nature of a covenant.

In the spiritual direction advocated in this book, directors try to make the alliance on the basis of a mutual acknowledgment that their purpose is to facilitate the directee's relationship with the Lord, that the indwelling spirit is the source of the directee's desire and effort to develop that relationship, and that there are forces within the directee which resist the Spirit's impetus. Spiritual direction, therefore, explicitly acknowledges what is often only implicit in other forms of pastoral care: that the directee's desire for more life, more integration, more union with God is grounded in the indwelling Spirit *and* that God is an active Other in the relationship. The working alliance is thus grounded in mystery and explicitly acknowledges that the way, too, is mystery. Any action of the director which seems to deny the mystery, for instance, by an a priori exclusion of some human experiences from the relationship with God ("We shouldn't be angry at

God"), or by authoritarian directions ("This week you will pray on your knees before the Blessed Sacrament"), is a failure to be faithful to the working alliance for spiritual direction as we understand it and may be fatal to the direction relationship.

Conflicting loyalties tend to interfere with the director's ability to listen. Conflicting loyalties also can affect the working alliance. An example may clarify our meaning: A married woman with two young children has come for spiritual direction to a nun who is a member of the parish team. The woman has had a rather robust prayer life and wants to remain close to God. She is, however, in a quandary because she has fallen in love with a divorced man. On several occasions recently they have come close to having intercourse. She cannot make sense of what is happening to her. She feels more alive than she has in years and even finds that her prayer life is more vital. She also feels guilty. She wants help to relate to God more deeply and to discover his will. The director agrees to work with her, but soon finds herself angry and upset because the woman does not seem to see the incongruity between her behavior and her state in life as a married woman and mother. In a supervisory session the director comes to see that another loyalty is keeping her from entering into an alliance with the woman: her sense of responsibility to the marriage bond and to the woman's husband and children. Instead of a working alliance she has an adversary relationship. Spiritual direction is impossible because the director has not been able to identify and ally herself with the woman's desire for growth in relationship to God. It is laudable to want to prevent infidelity in marriage, but spiritual directors have to leave that purpose to others. They cannot build a working alliance with a directee while maintaining hidden agenda. When doing spiritual direction, the director's primary loyalty is to the working alliance, a working alliance whose only purpose is the development of the relationship with the Lord.

It should not, however, be thought that the working alliance precludes raising questions with directees about the external

realities of their lives. In this example it would be appropriate
to ask how the woman reconciles her behavior with her Christian values and whether she speaks with the Lord of the relationship. The director could even share her own questions
about the compatibility of the relationship with a deep friendship with Jesus. She can only do this with profit for the spiritual direction, however, if she has a working alliance with the
woman and raises the questions in the context of that alliance.
The directee will be better able to hear the questions and also
to talk to the Lord about them if she knows that the director
is on her side and really wants to help her find God's will.
The criteria for discerning valid religious experience are used
to advantage in spiritual direction only when there is a working
alliance, because the use of these criteria may require the
raising of hard questions.

When examples like this come into discussions of spiritual
directors, someone will often ask: "Don't spiritual directors
have a responsibility to remind Christians of their obligations
in cases where directees are acting contrary to accepted Christian practices?" Our answer has to be a nuanced one. In the
first place, the directee usually knows that there is a discrep-
ancy. In the example, the married woman was disconcerted
by the exhilaration she felt when she also felt guilt. Secondly,
spiritual direction is only one of the many ministries of the
Church. We can presume that sermons, articles, newspaper
items, pastoral consultations are also part of the religious ambience of a directee. Thirdly, the issue is not whether the
director should or should not remind the directee of her obligations, but what the director's primary purpose is in any
intervention she makes. We believe that her primary purpose
is to foster the directee's relationship with God. It is enough,
therefore, that the director wants the directee to look at all
of her experience with freedom. But, finally, we presume that
God has an interest in the quality of the directee's life and
that behavior that is seriously inconsistent with God's desires
will lead to disturbances in the relationship with him. The

directee will feel distant from the Lord or uneasy; or she may withdraw from serious prayer; or her prayer will become flat and uninteresting. The director, whose working agreement has been to help her with prayer, can now begin to probe more deeply into the causes of the disturbance and thus help the directee become more discerning.

Thus, spiritual directors contribute immeasurably to the development of the working alliance by deciding clearly where their loyalties lie as well as by consistently and patiently considering the experiences in prayer reported by directees. They also contribute by everything they do that indicates that their primary concern is the directee's relationship with God.

People who come for spiritual direction will have many conflicting desires. The establishment of the working alliance helps them examine and order those desires. However, there are some attitudes and desires in directees that can make the working alliance difficult to establish.

In the last few years spiritual direction has become very popular in some parts of the world. The working alliance could be hindered by this sudden popularity. Some people could be seeking direction because it is "the thing to do." Unless that motivation changes, no working alliance can be achieved. Also, where direction is popular, certain directors may gain unusually high reputations. Under such circumstances, those who cannot get these directors may find it difficult to establish a working alliance with anyone else. Hidden resentment and distrust of the second-choice director's ability may preclude the establishment of a working alliance. Honest exploration of these feelings may be the only way to overcome the difficulty.

Again, where direction is popular and readily available, it may be sought as a substitute for something else—a willing ear or a counselor, for example. People have been known to seek spiritual direction because they could not bear the thought of seeking counseling or psychotherapy, or perhaps because they were unaware that therapy was what they needed. They may ostensibly agree to the contract of working with prayer experiences, but really be interested only in talking about problems they have with family, with community, with superiors, with work, with sex, with drink. The working alliance of spiritual direction is then never really established. Directors will have to decide what they want to do in such cases. They may want to continue some supportive pastoral care and help to sort out what is happening. They may decide that they do not have the expertise to deal effectively with at least some of these directees and work to help them to accept referral to a counselor or therapist.

Some people may seek direction in order to "save their vocation" or "their marriage." If in the course of the initial interviews this motive remains the dominant one, then the working alliance may never get established. Ultimately, the motivation for spiritual direction has to become the desire to grow in relationship with the Lord.

Often enough people come for spiritual direction with the avowed purpose of improving their prayer life. But when asked why they want to do so, their answer may run something like: "Because I'm a Christian," or "minister," or "a religious." Careful exploration is necessary to uncover whether such an answer means only: "I'm supposed to pray." There are many people who have never asked themselves whether they wanted to pray, whether they got anything out of prayer, why they wanted to pray. After careful exploration we find that some people really do not yet want to pray. We may then try to help them realize that they are free not to. God does not want from a free people a dumb submission to an uncomprehended law. The hope is that with a sense of freedom from an incomprehensible obligation such people will eventually find themselves desirous of prayer. We find that most people after careful exploration do deeply desire to pray, want to relate to the Lord, indeed hunger for prayer. They also find it a new experience to look at prayer as an inner desire, not simply an obligation imposed from without. Without the care and patience necessary to discover an intrinsic desire for prayer, the working alliance has a poor chance of being established. Directees may then never realize their own freedom before the Lord and before the spiritual director, and this freedom is the only ground on which authentic prayer can develop.

Finally, it sometimes happens (though more rarely nowadays) that people seek spiritual direction because they have been ordered or strongly advised to do so by someone in authority over them. The working alliance requires that directees have inner motivation for prayer and spiritual direction. People who have been "sent" to spiritual direction have to be worked with carefully in the beginning if a working alliance is to be established. In the more ordinary case motivation may be mixed; for example, when a novice or seminarian is expected to get spiritual direction and also wants it. However, careful discussion is necessary here, too, if a free working alliance is to develop.

The establishment of a working alliance is a necessary part of spiritual direction. Patient care at the beginning to establish this alliance of two peers working together for a common purpose is crucial to the development of a spiritual direction relationship that will be helpful to the directee's prayer and life. Lack of such care and attention can lead to a fuzzy agreement in which contradictory assumptions are held by the two parties. At worst, mutual recrimination can occur; at best, the relationship will peter out with little satisfaction to either party. Even with an explicit working alliance spiritual direction can be a difficult relationship to sustain; without it, the relationship becomes irksome or simply boring.

At this point the reader might find it helpful to consider a concrete case in which an agreement on spiritual direction is reached. A fifty-year-old priest has gained a reputation as a spiritual director. One day he receives a phone call from another priest who says he has heard about his work as a director and wants to explore the possibilities of direction for himself. They make an appointment to meet in the spiritual director's office.[9]

The priest arrives at the appointed time. After initial conversation that situates both parties comfortably, there might be a lull and the potential directee might say something like: "Well, I suppose I ought to explain why I'm here," or the director might say something like: "On the phone you said you were interested in spiritual direction." Where does the conversation go from here?

In the first place, the director wants to find out what brings the priest to his office; so he listens. The priest says that he has heard about spiritual direction from friends, especially from a nun who has found it very helpful. He is now forty years old and has been ordained for fifteen years. He has had his ups and downs with parish situations, but on the whole has enjoyed his life as a parish priest. He has especially liked working with adolescents in youth groups. Lately, though, he has been feeling more ill at ease, less sure of himself, lonely. The teenagers he works with grow up, marry, and leave the parish. A number of his friends in the priesthood have left active ministry and moved away. He doesn't have the zest for his work that he used to have. He feels spiritually dried-up and wonders what life will be like for the next twenty years if these feelings increase. He is attracted to some women he knows, especially to the nun who recommended that he come. He doesn't want to leave the priesthood, but he doesn't want to be a dried-up old man at fifty either. He is hoping that spiritual direction can help him revitalize his life.

The spiritual director asks what the priest understands by spiritual direction. He replies that he knows it has something to do with prayer and that he hopes it won't be like the direction he had in the seminary. The spiritual director agrees that spiritual direction does involve prayer and talking about experiences in prayer and then asks the priest how he prays and what he gets out of it. The point here is to establish what the person's experiences have been like and not to get a comprehensive account of his prayer life. The director wants to know what experiential foundations the spiritual direction can build on. If it turns out that prayer has been basically seen as an obligation and rarely experienced as enjoyable, then the director knows that he may well have to begin by helping the priest to understand prayer as a relationship freely entered into for the benefit of the person praying.

It might be helpful at this point to introduce some fictional dialogue to make the process more concrete. We shall illustrate two different approaches that the director (Tom) might take with the directee (Les).

Dialogue 1.

Tom: What would you be looking for from direction, Les?

Les: I guess just to be able to think about things a little more, maybe to get some ways of praying from you that would help me to get back on track. I say the breviary most days, but there may be some other ways of praying that would help.

Tom: You'd like me to make some suggestions?

Les: I guess so. You might want to suggest some Scripture passages, for example, that would get me going. Or some other ways of praying.

Tom: Well, we've talked about your background. I have a pretty good idea of what you're like and of your life experience. It sounds as though you need a renewal of your call. Why don't you think of taking the passage from the beginning of Jeremiah where Jeremiah hears the call of the Lord and begins to tell the Lord how he feels about the call? You might also think of taking the Last Supper account from John's gospel in which Jesus talks about priesthood and discipleship. Are there any others that you think it might be a good idea to take?

Les: No, I think those will keep me busy for a while.

Dialogue 2.

After Les's response to Tom's first question, Tom takes a different approach.

Tom: Could you tell me a little more about the way you have prayed?

Les: Well, I've used the breviary a lot and gotten a lot out of it. I find it a good form of prayer and I do it most of the time. Some days are better than others; some passages I don't get much out of.

Tom: Do you have any favorite passages?

Les: I don't think so; none I can think of right now. I like some of the Psalms and I like some of the selections from St. Paul.

Tom: Any passages that describe God to you better than others? Or describe the way you feel that he's relating to you better than others do?

Les: I can't think of any right now. St. Paul, maybe, but I can't think of any particular passages.

Tom: If I were to ask you what your clearest image of God is, the one that appeals to you most, what would you say?

Les: Well, it might be music. I enjoy listening to the stereo, hearing classical music. Music makes me feel calm and peaceful and at home. I feel stirred by it, warmed.

Tom: You feel at home, emotionally moved?

Les: Yeah; I've always loved music. When I was younger I liked country music a lot; now it's much more classical—Bach, Beethoven. I've developed a pretty good record collection.

Tom: The music says something to you about God?

Les: It reminds me that he's not an anthropomorphic figure, that he's all around me. It tells me that he wants me to be peaceful.

Tom: Peaceful?

Les: Not full of worry about work and the future but just kind of peaceful. I finish a day in which I've done a lot of worrying and I put on a record. That's what God is like for me.

Tom: He's the one who brings peace and relaxation, especially after worry and work?

Les: Yes, he's for me and with me.

Tom: That might be a good situation in which to begin prayer, Les. Listening to him bring peace to you and then letting yourself react to that. Perhaps saying to him how you feel about him bringing peace, how you feel about him relieving you of anxiety.

Les: I might feel a little dumb doing that. You mean saying something to him?

Tom: Yes. Just reacting to who he seems to be to you.

Les: What would that have to do with my feelings of uneasiness and frustration?

Tom: It might have something to do with it. It seems that it would
have something to do with you. You feel that seeing God as music
is a real way of seeing him. If you can react to him as he seems
to you, you might be able to speak to him about your other
feelings, like your frustration and uneasiness. Would you like to
try it?

Les: It's a bit strange to me, but I do know how much I need that
peace.

In the first dialogue the director rather quickly accepts Les's
desire for a program. Given Les's initial talk about his feelings
of uneasiness and spiritual dryness, Tom's suggestion of the
passage from Jeremiah and his reason for the suggestion are
plausible and insightful. But he makes two large assumptions:
that Les does experience God and that he does this most
easily through Scripture passages. In the second dialogue, the
director finds out something about Les's actual experience of
God and thus learns that the best entrée to relational prayer
for him is not, at least initially, through Scripture.

In this part of the interview the director is interested in the
present prayer life of the potential directee. In the initial
discussion we have just described he tries to estimate where
the potential directee is in his experience and understanding
of the relationship God offers. Before proceeding to establish
an agreement for spiritual direction, directors want to be sure
that there is a foundation for it, that the directee wants to
relate more personally to God. All the better, of course, if the
desire is to deepen a relationship already explicitly experienced and named, a fact the second approach brings to the
surface. Tom and Les can now proceed to discuss more precisely how they will work together.

To be really helpful spiritual direction takes time, at least
a few months, if not years. The length of time will be deter-
mined by circumstances of life such as the availability of director and directee to one another, the need of the directee
and the ability of the director to meet that need, and the
vicissitudes of the relationship between the directee and the
Lord.

The directee has a right to expect confidentiality from the director as well as a commitment to his growth in the relationship with the Lord. It is helpful for the director to spell out his understanding of confidentiality. Confidentiality should be very strict, but should not prevent the director from seeking competent supervision as long as the identity of the directee is protected. It is our practice to let directees know that we will not fill out evaluation forms or confidential records about them for third parties even if the directees themselves give permission for such evaluations. Our intent is to underline the fact that we want to serve the directee's relationship with God.

Privacy is another concern of directees. Directees need some assurance that they will not be overheard by others; hence, the room where the interviews occur ought to be so situated that others cannot, even inadvertently, overhear. Moreover, the sharing of inner experience is made more difficult if the directee feels that someone may walk through the room. It is embarrassing to be interrupted while weeping, for example, and the mere possibility of such an interruption may keep a directee from speaking about deeply emotional issues. Directees can also be offended if it seems that others—for example, the director's colleagues or members of his family—know too much about them and the reason why they seek out the spiritual director. It is difficult enough to disclose oneself to another; hence directors should do what they can to allay the fear that what directees disclose may become known to others.

Similarly, directees can legitimately be annoyed and angered if the director is continually interrupted by phone calls or knocks on the door. Arrangements can often be made before an interview that will make such interruptions unnecessary. If the director knows that he will be interrupted during an interview, he can explain this to the directee and apologize beforehand. If it is impossible to assure noninterruption, the director might discuss the problem with the directee so that he is aware of the director's own dilemma.

Director and directee should agree on how often they will meet. At the beginning of direction it often makes sense to meet weekly in order to get to know one another quickly, establish a strong working alliance, and get an appreciation of the rhythm of the directee's prayer life. After the initial period, say a month, they can evaluate the initial results of the direction and determine how often it would be best to meet.

The directee will be encouraged to set aside times to be consciously with the Lord and to pay attention to what happens when he is with the Lord. The experiences he has in these prayer times will be the main focus of the direction sessions. These prayer periods need to occur with some frequency and be of some length, but individuals have to discover the best rhythm for themselves. More important than either frequency or length of prayer periods is the attitude with which directees approach the time they give to prayer. Can they take the time as seriously as they would time spent with a close friend whom they want to know better? It can also help if they keep a journal or log in which after each time of prayer they briefly note what happened during it.

Besides regular attempts to pray, what else can the director expect of the directee? It seems to us that he can only ask a development of freedom, that is, that the directee move toward greater freedom to let the Lord be himself with him and to be himself with the Lord. If he asks anything else—that the person reach a certain level of prayer, that he become or remain a minister or priest, that she stay married, even that at this time he or she be a good person—he does so at the risk of confusing his own expectations with those of the Spirit, and so interfering with the Spirit's action. If, however, he implicitly asks only for freedom, and allows it to develop at the person's and the Lord's own pace, this expectation provides an encouraging and challenging atmosphere for the direction without presupposing particular results.

This is a pragmatic expectation. The director does not ask the directee to be more free than the directee wants to be, but he sees growth in freedom as the necessary atmosphere of direction. If the directee does not want more freedom at this point in his life, he must at least exercise his freedom by terminating the direction, either by breaking contact entirely or replacing direction with something else, perhaps some other form of pastoral care such as the occasional willing ear or advice-giving session, for instance.

One other factor that needs clarification is the question of fees. This can be a controversial and touchy topic. Our practice is not to accept fees for spiritual direction. It seems to us that it is one ministry that should be available to any Christian without concern for cost. Since spiritual direction is not, for the great majority of directors, a full-time occupation, they usually can offer this service gratis. We recognize that not everyone will agree with our stand, and we also realize that sound reasons can be adduced for a fee. We are only stating our practice and preference. If a fee is expected, however, the director should make this clear and talk it over with the directee. If none is expected, the director might well mention this fact. Money can be a thorny subject, and uncertainty about what is expected can bother a directee.

The elements of the agreement are all more or less explicit at this point of the initial interview. The directee should now be given some time to ponder what has been said. Even if he feels ready to make the decision for direction, it is wise to encourage reflection before he finally makes up his mind. He is about to take a fateful step, to begin what might become "a dark and dangerous journey" (even though its end is Rivendell).[10] T. S. Eliot puts it this way:

> But let me tell you, that to approach the stranger
> Is to invite the unexpected, release a new force,
> Or let the genie out of the bottle.
> It is to start a train of events
> Beyond your control. . . .[11]

It is well to insist on reflection before making the decision. Such insistence makes it clear that the directee has a free choice to make. It is critical that he be aware of his freedom from the beginning. If this atmosphere of growing freedom is present and is seen to be all that the director asks of the directee, the direction will not go stagnant because of the director's expectations and should avoid the danger of programming. It should, in other words, help the person open himself alertly and willingly to the living, unpredictable God rather than to any finite plan of life or prayer.

At the end of the initial interview—or interviews—the directee can be advised to ponder what has been discussed and then to call for an appointment if he wishes to begin. Here again, the freedom to begin or not is underscored, and he can without loss of face simply decide not to call.

In conclusion, the way one conceives of the relationship between director and directee follows from one's conception of the nature of spiritual direction. Because we conceive of spiritual direction as help given to another Christian to foster his relationship with the Lord, we believe that the relationship of director and directee is one of companionship. A unique kind of working alliance develops between director and directee, an alliance based on the agreement that the director will help the directee work toward what he wants—a closer relationship with the Lord.

Disturbances in the Relationship Between Director and Directee

Spiritual direction is an interpersonal process in which two people work together toward the goal of a deeper, more explicitly intimate and mutual relationship with God. This working together, if it is more than occasional and lasts a fairly long time, always brings about some degree of closeness between the people themselves. The two people become aware of one another and react to one another on a more personal level. They may pray for one another, care about one another's sicknesses and family difficulties if they know about them, have to work at mutual honesty, sometimes misunderstand one another and resent one another's failings, and have to talk out the misunderstanding and resentment. The relationship, in other words, if it is to be genuinely helpful to the directee, undergoes the vicissitudes of every relationship that is not completely impersonal.

Along with the usual difficulties involved in any personal relationship, however, there are other difficulties that arise in spiritual direction precisely because the purpose of spiritual direction is the growth of the directee. These special difficulties impede that growth and for that reason deserve special attention.

Earlier we spoke of the conflicting desires of directees that manifest themselves in resistance to growth in the relationship with the Lord. We mentioned that the relationship between director and directee can also be a source of disturbance to the directee's relationship with the Lord. The director's person, characteristics, and method of approach can become the focus of a directee's reactions. The director might then hear something like this: "There's nothing wrong with my prayer life that isn't just part of being human; the problem is that I'm not getting much out of you. You're not helping me enough and you seem to get upset with what I'm telling you." Or like this: "You've been a great help to my prayer life, but I don't know you at all. If it weren't for you, I'd be lost in life; you're the most important person in my life and I think we should talk about our relationship and get to know one another better as people."

Statements like these may not be signs of resistance, but resistance can express itself in these ways. We want now to examine those aspects of the relationship between director and directee that are impediments to the growth of the directee in his relationship with the Lord.

The purpose of spiritual direction is to foster the relationship between directees and their Lord. Thus, spiritual direction takes as its primary function to help the directee to open himself to the Lord and overcome his resistance to the mystery of God. The working alliance relies on the directee's impulses toward more reality, more life, more wholeness, more union with God—impulses whose ultimate source is the Spirit who dwells in our hearts. But precisely because directors, at least ideally, ally themselves with the indwelling Spirit and his impulses, they must expect that those impulses and desires which are frightened by mystery and thus are opposed to the process of contemplation and of spiritual direction will cause trouble not only with the directee's relationship with the Lord but also with the working alliance. Therefore when the resistance to the Lord is strong and the director is trying to help the directee to face the resistance and look at the Lord, the relationship to the director can become the lightning rod that attracts and seeks to ground the forces of resistance. Then the director becomes the focus of the directee's energies. The directee may begin to spend much of his prayer time and his time with the director ruminating about their relationship. He may feel positively or negatively toward the director, but the resistive nature of the focus on their relationship betrays itself in the fact that the directee has little or no time or energy left over for his relationship with the Lord. His preoccupation, in other words, conflicts with the purpose for which he came.

One of the most effective ways to resist growth in the relationship with the Lord is to distort the reality of the director. At the beginning of direction, the directee perceived the director as a helpful companion; now he organizes his perception so that the director seems to him like a harsh taskmaster, a tender mother, or some other figure from his past. This organizing is not consciously done, but it can be nonetheless real and can powerfully affect the contemplative prayer of the directee. In psychological counseling this distortion of perception has been termed *transference*. It can be defined as a reaction based on the assimilation of the director to an image derived from one's childhood.

Suppose that the transference reaction has positive affective tones. For example, the director, a woman twenty years older than the directee, a young man, begins to be perceived as the "good mother," with the directee reacting as the "dutiful son." Then the directee will try to please the director, will be looking for support and encouragement, will not want to think of "bad" feelings he has had. In prayer his main preoccupation will be with how pleased or displeased the director will be, not with the action of the Lord. It is easy to see that the real purpose of spiritual direction is successfully, even though unconsciously, avoided by such a transference reaction. If, instead, the image is negatively toned ("harsh mother–bad child"), then the directee may again be unable to tell the director the whole truth about himself and, of course, be unable to be himself before the Lord as well.

It will be important in the direction—even crucial—for the director to try to help the person to look at this interference. She might say, for example: "You haven't spoken in the last two weeks of the way the Lord seemed to be acting in your prayer a few weeks back. Has anything further been happening?" Or she may ask, if the prayer has for some time been featureless, "Do you recall the last time you prayed when the Lord seemed present and active to you? What did he seem like then? Do you think he still wants to be that way with you?" The director thus asks the directee to identify the mainstream of his prayer and to speak of his present reactions to it. In this way she establishes a context within which the transference reaction can be purposefully discussed.

For those readers whose acquaintance with the psychological meaning of transference is minimal, a brief theoretical interlude may be helpful. Freud is generally credited with the definition and elucidation of the concept of transference. However, transference phenomena were known prior to Freud.[1] Those who treated "nervous" individuals often became aware of strong and inappropriate love and hate reactions to themselves, but these were regarded simply as nuisances or as unavoidable and sometimes messy concomitants of the treatment of these patients. Freud's contribution was to look closely at these phenomena and then to make them the vehicle of the "cure" or growth of the person being treated. His theory of neurosis presupposes that the neurotic individual carries around inside himself ways of perceiving self and others (self-other schemata) and of behaving that are self-defeating and ultimately harmful to all the person's important relationships. These ways of perceiving and behaving are learned early in life and continue to influence relationships even when the person is an adult. Freud saw that transference reactions in therapy were manifestations of these underdeveloped personality patterns. The patient reacts to the therapist in the same self-defeating and inappropriate ways that get him into trouble in other areas of his life. Because of the working alliance, the therapist can help the patient to see what he is doing to himself and to realize that he does not have to distort reality in this way. Through the relationship with the therapist he can learn more appropriate adult ways of perceiving and behaving—that is, his self-other schemata become more mature, flexible, and differentiated.[2]

Psychoanalysis as a therapy is impossible if the client cannot allow himself to experience transference reactions; it is also impossible if the client cannot at the same time maintain a working alliance with the analyst. In the former case there would not be enough to "analyze" for the growth to occur; in the latter, the client could not work with the analyst to "analyze" the transference reactions and overcome them. The balance is a delicate one since transference reactions are the most persistent of the resistances that the client puts up to evade the growth for which he has entered the working alliance. In psychoanalysis resistance is not only expected but is welcomed as a sign that the process is going well.

Psychoanalytic therapy, therefore, is a relationship therapy. The growth and development occur in and through the relationship to the therapist. The analyst needs to develop a strong working alliance with the client that will allow the client to regress in the therapeutic hour—that is, allow him to bring his self-defeating modes of relating to others into the therapeutic relationship itself in order to defeat them. The analyst, in other words, through the working alliance helps the client to keep a strong grip on present reality while at the same time allowing and even encouraging the neurosis to surface in the relationship in the form of a transference neurosis. A transference neurosis means what it says: the client's whole neurotic, fixated, and defensive way of being and behaving reveals itself in the analytic hour, and the analyst counts on his own integrity not to respond to this self-defeating mode of behavior by behaving in kind (thereby reinforcing the neurosis); he also counts on the working alliance to enable the client to overcome the massive resistance to change that the neurosis is.

Many kinds of therapy and counseling involve a similar dynamic, we believe, if their purpose is to enable the client through this relationship (of counseling or therapy) to develop more appropriate, mature, and fulfilling ways of being human and of relating to people and the world. We would include among such therapies and counseling the more mediating forms of pastoral care. The relationship to the counselor, therapist, helper, priest, or minister is the vehicle through which the person learns a new and more fulfilling way to be human, to live, to look at self and others; that is, he learns new self-other schemata. The differences in the various theories whose aim is not manipulation, however enlightened, but growth in freedom appear to lie not in the dynamic itself but in the depth to which transference phenomena are fostered. Transference, in other words, is ubiquitous in counseling and therapy; the depth of regression fostered in the various theories varies widely.

We will now turn to some of the conditions that foster the regression that transference entails, so that spiritual directors will understand better their own role as spiritual directors.

The more ambiguous counselors and therapists are, the more clients will relate to them out of their own past experience.[3] The less I know about you, about your expectations, about your reactions to me, the more I will relate to you on the basis of my past experience, since I have little else to go on. Some therapists remain very ambiguous, others much less so. Classical psychoanalysts are probably the most ambiguous of all, seeing themselves as "blank screens" upon which clients can project their past experience. They sit behind the client so that their faces cannot be seen. They give only one basic rule for what is to be said by the client: "Say anything that comes to mind." Nothing could be more ambiguous as a requirement. They try not to influence the "free associations" of their clients by any indication that some associations are good, others less so.

The use of the couch in psychoanalysis fosters regression not only because it keeps the analyst out of view but also because of the recumbent position itself and the utterance of anything that comes to mind. The frequency of meetings has an effect on the intensity of the transference reactions. The more often client and therapist meet, the more intense and all-encompassing the transference becomes. Here again, psychoanalysis shows its consequentiality by scheduling appointments four to six times a week.

Although some therapists foster transference reactions, we believe that spiritual directors should not do so. Counselors foster transference reactions to themselves because they see the relationship to themselves as the primary vehicle for growth and development. The relationship that is fostered in spiritual direction is the relationship not of the director and directee, but of the directee and the Lord; the directee's personal growth and development will occur primarily through this latter relationship. Spiritual direction aims to help the directee to enter into a more profound relationship with the Lord where transference reactions to him can be faced and overcome by the Lord's own reality.[4] As these underdeveloped ways of relating oneself to the Lord change, so too do one's ways of relating self to others and to life in general. But the vehicle of change is fundamentally the relationship between the directee and the Lord.

Since spiritual directors do not intend to foster transference reactions to themselves, they tend to be less ambiguous about themselves than counselors are. In the concrete this means that they do not remain incognito, that they are rather companions on the way than unknown quantities. They answer questions about themselves as these come up, speak about their own experiences insofar as this seems helpful to the spiritual direction they are doing, and let directees see how they react and feel. At the same time, they should be mindful of the agreement and the working alliance they have with their directees. Directees come to directors for help with their prayer and not for friendship. Moreover, the director's experience should not become normative for the directee nor should it be so obtrusively offered that it delays the development of the directee's own sense of religious identity. Extensive self-disclosure by a director may be a sign of countertransference or of a failure to understand what spiritual direction means. The point remains, however, that spiritual directors are much more companions than the "blank screens" that psychoanalysts make of themselves.

In spiritual direction the likelihood of transference reactions is diminished by the focus of the discussions themselves. Directees are encouraged to focus primarily on their experiences in prayer. The focus is clear and less ambiguous than in therapy or counseling.

Spiritual directors usually meet directees at most once a week and frequently less often. Hence, the depth and intensity of transference reactions which develop when more frequent meetings are scheduled are less likely to occur. The directed (one-on-one) retreat, and especially the thirty-day directed retreat, is a special case, since the directee meets the director daily to talk about prayer experiences and to receive help in grasping what is happening in the prayer. In this situation strong transference reactions are more likely to occur than in ordinary spiritual direction. For the directed thirty-day retreat particular preparation is necessary. Ideally, only the more experienced and well-supervised directors engage in such retreats, and supervision during such retreats is particularly important. Those who make these retreats should be carefully selected for their relative maturity and their already proven capacity to pray in a contemplative way.

Everything about the setting and the interaction between director and directee in spiritual direction should emphasize the relationship with the Lord as the directee's most significant channel for growth. To state the contrast between spiritual direction and counseling as starkly as possible: in spiritual direction all transference reactions of directees should occur in the relationship with the Lord, not in the relationship with the director. Moreover, all resistances should come in prayer, not during the sessions of spiritual direction. All challenges and all confrontations of the directee should take place there as well. Admittedly, no such pure instances exist, but we put the case this starkly for the sake of clarity. Spiritual directors, therefore, try to avoid any action or setting or technique that would foster transference reactions to themselves. Most spiritual directors have no training in the management of the transference, and this is another important reason for caution. But the primary reason for not fostering transference reactions to themselves is that such reactions divert their directees from the relationship with the Lord.

We must, however, also say that transference reactions toward spiritual directors are unavoidable and are one of the usual vehicles for resistance to the process of contemplative prayer. Directors tend to be seen, for one thing, as authority figures, and directees will react to them out of their past experience with authority figures. Priests often have the added aura of the title "Father" to contend with and so will encounter the expectations directees have built up from their experiences with their own fathers and with all authority figures. Women directors will be the objects of feelings that have been stored up from past experiences, especially childhood experiences, with mothers, aunts, and teachers. Moreover, the simple fact that directees share intimate experiences with directors will tend to evoke personality patterns developed from dealings with those ambivalently experienced people of childhood in whom one wanted, often fearfully, to confide and who may have failed to understand. Transference reactions are, thus, inevitable in the work of spiritual direction.

How do we recognize the presence of such reactions? Transference reactions betray themselves by their intensity and inappropriateness; the spiritual director does not deserve the intense love, the intense anger, or the intense dependence that the directee feels towards him. A woman director, for example, may be thoughtful and kind and so deserve the affection of a directee; but if much of the directee's prayer time is spent in daydreaming about her and telling the Lord how grateful he is for her, then the reaction is too intense and inappropriate not to be suspected of transference.

Transference reactions are also marked by strong ambivalence. The directee both depends on and condemns the director at almost the same time. As a result, transference reactions are often capricious; if the director wonders, almost from moment to moment, what the attitude of the directee toward him and the process of direction is, he can suspect transference. The director also has good reason to suspect the presence of transference when the directee spends most of his prayer time or most of his spiritual direction time on the relationship to the director. It can be, of course, that the director by his own errors and countertransference has brought this on. But if he has not been responsible for the reactions, except by doing his job well and thus allowing resistance to God to come to a head, then he has reason to think that transference reactions are occurring because the directee is not attending to what he wanted from spiritual direction.

When transference feelings arise, the person at whom they are directed may well be dismayed and frightened at the intensity of the reaction and begin to wonder what he did wrong. "Have I been seductive and given this person the impression that I would be more than a companion on the way? After all, I have enjoyed his zest, his looks, his smile." "Is he so angry because I asked the wrong questions or made the wrong suggestions?" "Is the anger a response to the feelings of impatience I had at the last meeting?" "Do I belong in this work at all?" Directees are keen observers, and when transference reactions occur in them, they tend to use what they have observed in the director to make their reactions plausible. They do not do it consciously; this is the ordinary human way of making sense out of untoward and unpleasant experiences. Spiritual directors will have to remember that their normal human reactions, either of warmth and enjoyment or of anger and impatience, are insufficient reason for the intensity of affect that characterizes transference reactions. For spiritual direction to proceed successfully and help the directee, directors must calmly continue the dialogue with the directee and not waste time blaming themselves.

An example: the director is a man in his late forties, the directee a woman about thirty-five. From their first meetings the director has sensed a strong hostility in the directee which alternates with openness and trust. Attempts to discuss the hostility are met by a denial of its presence. The prayer seems to be going well enough, yet the director feels that there is something missing, something that does not ring true. The director wonders whether he is causing the hostility, since the warmth he usually feels for directees is not present in his interviews with this woman.

Only much later does the real reason emerge. From the beginning of the direction the room used for the interviews reminded the directee of a particularly unpleasant experience of childhood and brought back strong anger and fear. She transferred those feelings onto the present situation with the director. The feelings aroused were so strong that she could not deal with them either in prayer or in the direction sessions. The director, in his tendency to blame himself, failed to take into account the intensity of the affect he intuited and the inappropriateness of that much angry feeling directed toward himself. In this instance, too, the resistance was so strong that the director's questions about the anger led nowhere, perhaps with good reason. The anger was probably so explosive that the directee could not look at it until her trust in God and the director had been built up through considerable experience.

How do spiritual directors deal with transference reactions? Quick analyses and technical jargon are not helpful; for example, "You must have been angry at your father," or "That sounds like transference to me," or "Well, you know that such love reactions are unrealistic and are not really aimed at me; I'm just the target because I'm helping you." The other extreme would be to ignore the transference reactions entirely and ask: "How has your prayer been?" or "Have you taken these feelings (of love or anger toward the director) to the Lord?" Such reactions will appear defensive, and no doubt they are.

It is not easy to describe a middle course, or to take one in the actual situation. But let us attempt an example. The directee is a twenty-eight-year-old divinity student, the director a forty-year-old married woman. The direction is in its sixth month, and the director has begun to notice that the student drops by her office and her home more than usual recently, seems more animated in the sessions, prolongs the sessions by talking about shows he has seen and people he has met. She also has noticed that he does not say much about his prayer and that when he does he talks about prayers of gratitude, especially for her presence in his life. Finally, he tells her that he loves her, that she is the first woman who has ever understood him, and that he would like to get to know her better. How should she handle the situation?

The director must first of all be aware of her own feelings. She probably is at least somewhat flattered by the affection. If she has a sense of perspective and humor and enough gratification in her own life, she will feel the incongruity and inappropriateness of the reaction to her. She will also wonder whether these reactions are preventing the student from praying and are thus being used by his tendency to resistance.

We suggest a straightforward approach to the directee. In real life the response would never be said this crisply and clearly, perhaps, or all at once, but one way of replying might be: "I'm touched by your affection; what woman wouldn't be? And I'm sure that it has been difficult for you to bring this up and talk about it. But I'm also wondering how your prayer has gone since we last met." What she may find out is that when he tries to pray, all he does is think about her and tell the Lord how grateful he is that she is in his life. Then the director can begin to help him to see how his absorption with her is preventing him from listening to the Lord. They may well discover that the absorption with her has occurred at a critical point in his prayer life. For example, it may be that a challenge to his life style has been emerging from his contemplation of Jesus. The transference reaction serves his resistance, that part of him that does not want to face the Lord's challenge. The director thus remains faithful to the working alliance with him by helping him understand better what is happening to him in his prayer and his life.

In this example the reaction is open and clearly observable; more often, transference reactions are not so clearly expressed. Directors sense that something is wrong; they may, for instance, notice missed appointments, silence, a grudging and bare description of how prayer and life are going, argumentativeness. Here again, straightforwardness is the best policy. If a director believes that the person's prayer life is being affected or wonders whether it is, he should indicate this. He should not interpret, but raise a question for reflection. If the directee denies that anything is wrong, it does little good to pursue the subject. Pursuit will look like badgering or a search for proof that the director was correct all along. A question gives the directee a chance to think, and if the director's intuition is accurate, he may then recognize its accuracy. Moreover, if the prayer is being affected, this fact will also surface more clearly and the directee will have to come to terms with it. Directors do their best work when they maintain their attitude of companionship and raise questions for reflection rather than play the detective or the archaeologist of the spirit.[5]

Let us take one more example. The director (John), is a fifty-five-year-old Presbyterian pastor, the directee (Dave), a parishioner, a recent widower and the father of two small children. They have been working together for about four months. Dave's wife died eight months ago and a few months

later he came to talk to John about the emptiness of his life
and his desire to do something about it. After a couple of
meetings they agreed that spiritual direction was appropriate
to Dave's concerns. Dave was a devout man but had a relatively undeveloped prayer life. When he realized that after
the death of his wife (Kate) he could not pray, he was afraid
that he was losing his faith as well as his interest in life. At
least for the sake of his children, he felt, he wanted to do
something about it. Gradually Dave was able to develop a
contemplative kind of prayer in which he learned to listen to
the Lord and express his concerns to the Lord. At first he
found great comfort in this prayer. He felt the Lord's concern
and care for himself and his children. Isaiah 40, "Comfort,
comfort my people. . ." meant a great deal to him. He cried
while reading it in prayer and again while telling John about
the prayer experience.

But sometime during the third month of direction Dave's
prayer begins to go dry. The Lord seems very distant and
Dave finds himself distracted and bored with prayer. When
John tries to find out in more detail what is happening, Dave
just shrugs. "Now that I'm feeling better, I'm a lot busier and
my mind is caught up with details of work, the kids and the
house. I guess I'm bound to be distracted." And he seems
disinclined to explore things further. But John does note a
hint of anger as Dave talks about how busy he is and asks him
whether he is angry. "I don't feel angry—and I really have
nothing to be angry about."

The next time they meet Dave again reports dryness and
distractions, and the irritation seems even stronger. John asks
Dave how he feels about the dryness. "It's not the best thing
in the world, but from what I've read, dryness in prayer is
to be expected." "That may be true enough," John says, "but
that doesn't mean we can't have feelings about it." "Well,
suppose I don't like it, what can I do about it? I've done my
best, I still keep trying to pray—and I've really got too many
things to do right now to do any more or to worry about my
prayer."

John tries to explore Dave's feelings but to no avail, and he senses a growing anger in Dave toward him. "It sounds as though you may be getting irritated at me, Dave?" "No, I'm not angry, but I do wish you'd stop badgering me with all these questions right now." "I don't mean to badger, Dave; I just thought it might help to look more closely at your feelings in prayer." "I know you mean well, but right now I'm just too harried to concentrate and your questions are just making me more harried." The meeting ends soon after. John was at a loss as to what to do to help and even wondered whether he was being too intrusive. After consultation, however, he felt better about his approach and less inclined to blame himself.

Two weeks later Dave returns. It is obvious to John that he is very angry and upset. The dialogue goes like this.

Dave: We're not getting anywhere. I feel I'm wasting your time. I've decided to call it quits.

John: What's happened, Dave?

Dave: Nothing's happened. That's the problem. And I'm sick and tired of being made to feel like a religious retard.

John: A religious retard?

Dave: Just because you can sit on your backside here all day and read books on prayer and have the leisure to pray doesn't give you the right to look down your nose at us lay folk.

John: What makes you feel that I look down on you?

Dave: Oh, Come on! Just because I'm busy and get distracted in prayer, you act as though I were a Neanderthal. All those damned questions about anger. Well, I am angry—at you and your holier-than-thou attitudes. What do you know about what it's like to lose your wife and have to bring up two kids and work hard at the office?

John: You're obviously very angry at me, Dave. And you seem to feel that my questions or probes about your anger were a put-down. Can you tell me what gave you that impression?

Dave: What were you asking me about anger for? Even if I were angry, what's so wrong about that?

John: Let me assure you that I was not asking about anger to put you down. You may not believe me, but I know I didn't feel any kind of negative judgment. I thought I sensed anger in your voice, and I wondered if you were angry about anything. But you seem to have taken my questions as a judgment on you.

Dave: Yes, I did. It was as though you were saying: Be a man and take your cross and carry it.

John: Well, I don't know where that came from because I didn't feel that way. I thought you might be angry at God or life and that you had every right to be. And if you were angry, and didn't know it or couldn't express it, I felt that might be the reason for your dryness.

Dave: But how can you be angry at God? Look at all that he's done for me. But I tell you, as we talk, I begin to feel some anger. I feel like I'm left holding the bag. I've got to keep working, I feel all alone, and I've got the kids to take care of. But who am I to blame? I feel like a damn fool getting angry at Kate—but to tell you the truth I do feel that she left me in the lurch. And where the hell was this God of comfort when we really needed him?

The example is compressed, but such reactions do occur. The director could have become angry and fought with Dave; or he could have become apologetic about his intrusiveness. In either case, he might never have found out what was really troubling Dave. In the example, he is not overwhelmed by the anger. In real life he probably would have taken more time to explore Dave's anger at him. But he realizes that the anger is inappropriate, maintains his composure and the working alliance and helps Dave look at his anger and the real sources of it. Now he can also help him express these feelings directly to the Lord. It seems clear that Dave was faced with a new step in his relationship with the Lord, the step of expressing "negative" feelings about him, and that he found this step very difficult. John's attempts to help him look at his feelings led to him becoming the lightning rod for the anger and fear. His ability to handle the transference reaction, however, helped Dave to take the next step.

Spiritual directors are before all else human beings. They too, therefore, will not be immune to carrying over (or transferring) unfinished business from their past lives, especially from their childhood, to their dealings with people in the present. They will be especially prone to do so in those situations that put their own personalities to the test. Spiritual directors find that the work of direction, especially with certain directees, brings them face to face with their own relationship with the Lord and their tendencies to resist that relationship. Under such circumstances, the tendency to transfer may well be activated as a vehicle for their own resistance.

An example will illustrate how countertransference[6] can affect spiritual direction. A priest about forty-five years old is giving spiritual direction to a married woman with a family. He has been helpful to her, and she has grown in intimacy with the Lord. As she becomes more sure of God's love for her, she also becomes more free of a kind of awe of priests. She is an intelligent, intuitive person, and she begins to see how women, including herself, are treated as second-class members of the Church. She begins to experience strong anger in her prayer. It is directed at the hierarchy and priests, but also at God for allowing the discrimination. As she tries to tell her director about her experiences in prayer, he gets very upset and accuses her of a lack of humility and a desire for power rather than service. The woman is struck dumb and begins to doubt all her experiences of God. She feels ashamed and never returns for direction to the priest.

In this case we have elements that indicate the presence of countertransference. The director's response is disproportionate, inappropriate, and punitive.[7]

One of the more troublesome characteristics of countertransference reactions is that they can go unnoticed for a long time. Many spiritual directors do not seek out supervision. The priest in the example might, therefore, never be forced to reflect on his reaction. The fact that the woman does not return for direction can be seen by the director as a sign that she is proud and cannot face honest confrontation. Even if the director is being supervised, he may, quite unconsciously, avoid talking about this instance because there are other, "more interesting ones," he has had. And who can blame him?

To become conscious of countertransference reactions is to bring on pain and anxiety. But, as we have seen, the directee suffers and so, too, in a more subtle way, does the director who avoids the truth.

It should be clear that not all emotional reactions to directees are countertransference reactions. Emotions such as affection, warmth, anger, and sadness can occur in directors and may need to be dealt with by them. The reactions we call countertransference, however, are at once strong and disproportionate, somewhat like a day-long depression triggered by the postman telling you that you forgot a stamp. Such reactions indicate that the director's own unresolved emotional conflicts are interfering with the process of spiritual direction. None of us is immune from such reactions, especially in work that draws on the deepest wellsprings of our own grappling with Mystery. This is the basic reason for seeking competent supervision, the kind that will enable us to reflect honestly on what we are doing and why we are doing it.

What can directors do to protect their directees from countertransference reactions? It is very helpful to reflect on one's reactions after each session of spiritual direction and especially to take careful note of unusual affective reactions, such as strong anger or warmth or no affective response at all. One might also note whether prayer experience was the focus of the session. Such reflection can provide the material for a supervisory discussion about one's work. Occasionally, too, directors might look over the list of their directees to see whether they are avoiding supervisory discussion of the relationship with any of them. Such avoidance can be a sign that there is a difficulty in the relationship. They might also monitor their own dreams or daydreams occasionally to see whether one directee stands out there. The purpose of such self-examination is not to unnerve oneself but to be open to possible blind spots or resistance.

One almost universal conflict for those of us in helping professions is the conflict between the need to be helpful and the need to be helped. We can unconsciously hope to gain the love, respect, and warmth we need by nurturing others, by being available to people who need help. The counter-transference aspects of such a hope show themselves in too much concern for directees, too much desire for their progress and their enjoyment of prayer, and in resentment and a sense of loss when they do not seem to care or do not "improve." Competent supervision can help a director to recognize this tendency and to ask the Lord to free him of this need or at least to moderate it.

Suppose that in supervision a woman director discovers a radical dislike for a directee that is based on her own past experiences with a younger brother and that the dislike is one she cannot neutralize. Let us also suppose that the dislike is not altogether a projection—that is, that the person has un-likable qualities. Unless the director can ally herself with the healthy and grace-inspired side of the directee, she cannot be helpful to him in spiritual direction. It may not, however, be easy to refer him to someone else, both because he would take the referral as a rejection and because the next director might find him unlikable too. The director will then have to rely on asking for the grace to see him with the eyes of the Lord and also on praying that she be healed of the bitterness that makes it difficult for her to see the good in this man. She may also need to seek spiritual direction more intensely her-self. Finally, she may find that she needs psychological coun-seling to overcome the block.

Ultimately, if the director cannot come to a positive alliance with the directee, she must, for the directee's sake (and per-haps for her own too) try to persuade him to see someone else. If she does this, she will have to make it clear that she is at least partly to blame for the impasse. But it is important to remember that we are now talking about a case in which the director has recognized her own countertransference problems. Directors should not accuse themselves of fanciful personal difficulties if they see that the problem is really the directee's unwillingness to use spiritual direction for his growth and development.

The best criterion directors can use as a touchstone for determining whether their feelings toward directees are appropriate or not is the question: Are these feelings consonant with the development of their own contemplative attitude toward God and toward their directees? The contemplative attitude toward directees' descriptions of what is happening in their prayer is essential to good direction. When that attitude is interfered with, directors have to seek the reasons for the interference. A director might be resisting a new experience of God as he listens to a directee; he might also be experiencing the effect of unresolved emotional conflicts. Directors need to do whatever is necessary to maintain their contemplative attitude if they notice that they are in danger of losing it.

11

Supervision in Spiritual Direction

The relationship with God, we have stressed, is the central fact of a Christian's spiritual life, and it is in order to develop that relationship that a person approaches a spiritual director for help. When he does so, he enters into a relationship with the director that has for its purpose the facilitating of the relationship with God. These statements are simple enough, and the relationships they describe may seem simple too. Basically they are. But relationships between persons are never static. They change. They can grow—become broader, richer, more nourishing. They can also weaken—become pale, attenuated, confused, and aimless. These changes are sometimes the result of conscious reflection and deliberate choice. But frequently they come about without our recognizing the factors responsible for the changes that are occurring.

Spiritual directors give a great deal of thought and energy to promoting the sound development of the relationship between director and directee. In our experience one of the best ways to promote this sound development is supervision.

The concept of supervision is new in the field of spiritual direction, but the reality to which the concept points has not been entirely unknown.[1] Even though the reality existed, however, the practice of supervision does not seem to have received much reflection and systematic development, nor until recent years does it seem to have been widespread.

Even where it was practiced, the focus was on the problem or on the person with the problem, not on the spiritual director himself. Today, however, supervision is being taken more seriously in all areas of pastoral care as pastoral care learns from the development of the theory and practice of supervision in the fields of psychiatry, psychology, and social work. In these fields, the focus of supervision is on the person being supervised and on his or her growth as a helping person, since the basic purpose of supervision of counselors or therapists is to help them to become more therapeutic.[2]

Our adaptation of this paradigm holds that supervision of spiritual directors aims at helping them to become in turn more helpful in promoting other people's relationship with God—in other words, to help them become more able spiritual directors. Just as the relationship of director to directee is one of the best means for facilitating the directee's growth in the relationship with God, so too the relationship of supervisor to spiritual director is one of the best means of facilitating the director's growth as a director.

Supervisors, like spiritual directors, are human beings, and human beings tend to be consistent in the way they structure or schematize similar realities. If consistency is the hobgoblin of little minds, it is also unconsciously the way all minds seem to work. If I see spiritual direction as advice-giving, supervision for me will also be an advice-giving project. If spiritual direction for me means helping the directee make sense of his life experience, especially as it impinges on his relationship to God, then supervision will also tend to be an exploration of experience. Indeed, the way one does spiritual direction will probably be the way one does supervision of spiritual direction. It should therefore come as no surprise that our view of supervision has affinities with our view of spiritual direction.

Just as we look upon the religious experience of the directee as the foodstuff of spiritual direction, so too we see the experience of directors qua directors as the foodstuff of supervision. If the spiritual director wants help to become a more competent director, then he and his supervisor must focus on what happens between him and his directees in the time of spiritual direction—that is, on the experience the director has had of doing spiritual direction.

The question of focus is as important for supervision as it is for spiritual direction, and for the same reason. If spiritual directors do not focus on the religious experience of their directees, then this most intimate and challenging area of experience will ordinarily be skirted in their conversations. Other areas of life experience, and especially problem areas, will take up the time. Directees may get help with these areas, but they may not develop a deeper personal relationship with the Lord. So too, if supervisors do not focus on the experience itself of giving direction, then that experience will get short shrift.

There is at least one other similarity between supervision and direction itself. Just as spiritual direction addresses the faith life of the directee, so too its supervision addresses the faith life of the spiritual director. In spiritual direction the director concentrates on the directee's experiences with the Lord and on his resistance to those experiences. In the same way, the supervisor of a spiritual director concentrates on the director's experiences as a director and the lived beliefs that color his responses to the directee.

When directors ask for supervision, they may have a variety of purposes in mind. They may be perplexed by a particular directee; they may need reassurance that they are doing competent work; they may, half-consciously, want to find out how the supervisor would direct a particular person. All of these purposes, while perhaps legitimate and even attainable in a supervisory relationship, are, we believe, peripheral to the main issue. The primary purpose of supervision is the personal growth of the spiritual director as spiritual director. Therefore directors who seek supervision in this model are not at bottom asking for help with technique or with spiritual diagnosis or with the proper use of scriptural texts. They are asking for help to become someone.

Directors in this situation are thus opening themselves to challenge and growth, and they approach such an enterprise with some trepidation. When we present our work, but especially when we present ourselves, to the scrutiny of others, we are putting ourselves on the line, and no one with any sense does this without some fear of being found wanting. If, moreover, the supervisor also has authority to pass or fail directors in a training program, the anxiety tends to be even greater. At the same time, if supervision is to be helpful so that directors do become more competent, they must run these risks and present their experience as honestly as possible. Obviously, directors who do so need a great deal of trust in the supervisor, in themselves, and in the Spirit who gives life.

Indeed, this type of supervision requires trust on both sides. Supervisors must trust the capacity and desire of their supervisees to develop as knowledgeable, competent, and confident facilitators of other people's relationship with God. If they do not develop such trust (at least more trust than mistrust) during the early stages of supervision, they will communicate their negativity at least by their attitude, if not also by their overt behavior. They may angrily question supervisees or coolly point out mistakes. Supervisees will not experience them as on their side, but rather as opponents or judges. None of these feelings need be overt or even recognized by either person, but the atmosphere they create will be at least somewhat noxious to growth. In these circumstances, some spiritual directors in supervision tend to feel more and more self-doubt; they dread supervision and doubt their capacity to do spiritual direction. Others react with anger and a posture of self-defense before the supervisor. In either case, growth as a director is achieved only with difficulty—and the supervision is not the vehicle for such growth.

Supervisees, too, have to grow in trust. Otherwise, they will hesitate to present their actual experience as directors;

they will put their best foot forward and will try to figure out what the supervisor wants to hear and then give him that. Before trust develops, concepts are used to conceal experience rather than reveal it; phrases like "contemplative attitude" and "take it to the Lord" are used but sound hollow and empty of experiential content.

We do well to recall that individuals grow and change as persons through relationships with others and that the amount of growth depends on the quality and depth of the relationship involved. Growth as a spiritual director cannot be superficial; it must take root in the core of the person, in the heart, in that center where directors meet God and other people most intimately. They must develop as persons whose hearts are open and discerning, whose faith, hope, and love are almost tangible. To develop in this way, they have to relate to God and also to their supervisor in depth. They must risk exposure of the strengths and limitations of their hearts, their minds, their faith, their hope, and their love to the supervisor. No one does this lightly; any director can only gradually develop such trust in another human being. So the supervisor and the supervisee need to take time with one another to develop this kind of trust. Moreover, the achievement of an in-depth relationship of trust is not a once-for-all event. Such a relationship is alive; it shifts and moves as new levels of trust and distrust are touched. But its general trend, if it is to be most helpful, is toward deeper trust.

Each supervisory relationship will differ precisely because the persons differ; the way any two people interact is unique. With one supervisee, a supervisor may find himself rather passive, seeing no need to intervene frequently, because the supervisee is aware of his experience and easily able to share it. The supervisor may spend more time helping him to understand the meaning of his experience. With another supervisee, he may find himself working very differently, intervening frequently with questions about gestures, words, feelings because the supervisee is relatively unaware of certain aspects of his experience. It may even be that certain types of supervisors (for example, the more intuitive) are better suited to supervising certain types of directors (for example, the more rational), because of the complementarity involved. Whether or not this is true, it is nevertheless true that each supervisory relationship is unique.

At the same time, when trust is present, the working alliance of supervision is based on the same premise in all instances. The purpose of supervision is the becoming of a spiritual director. Both parties have to agree that growth as a director is what is sought even though such growth, like knowledge, may make a bloody entrance. It must be explicit that the one seeking supervision wants to grow as a director and to find out whether he or she is suited for this pastoral ministry. The supervisor needs to know this as much as does the supervisee; when he knows that the supervisee wants this, he will have more trust in the relationship and be more supportively challenging. The supervisee must know that he can count on the supervisor's working alliance with him so that he can reveal some of his deepest fears and most troubling experiences and responses. When a solid working alliance has been established either between an individual director and a supervisor or among a group of directors meeting for mutual supervision, it is far more likely that the supervisee will present his most troubling experiences for help. And it is the troubling experiences that most often reveal the growing edge of faith and ability as a director.

The following fictionalized description of the process of forming a working alliance may be helpful.

The supervisor (John) and the supervisee (Rose) knew very little of one another prior to beginning the year of supervision, but they had heard positive reports of one another. As the year began, they participated in a faith experience weekend prior to the choice of supervisors. John recalls: "I was touched by Rose's courage in facing her demons and by her willingness to talk about God in the concrete." Rose says: "I was surprised to see John cry, and I was positively impressed by that and by the simple way he talked about God." After she chose him as her supervisor, Rose told John: "I chose you as supervisor for another reason too: you seem to be the kind of person who will confront feelings directly, and I need that kind of help. I'm not very good at expressing my feelings." This kind of courage and honesty helped John to trust Rose and to be himself with her. In their first meeting they shared these reasons for wanting to work together and also the expectations they had of each other. They agreed that their task together was to help Rose to develop as a spiritual director.

John: It was important that we agree on this purpose. There are lots of times when I'd rather do other work or watch a ball game or daydream than do the sometimes hard work of supervision. Without that firm agreement with Rose, I would have often politely avoided hard questions and delicate areas.

Rose: It was very important for me, especially in the early stages, that we had explicitly agreed on our purpose. John had to keep reminding me of it because I kept looking for techniques and texts of Scripture to suggest to directees. It took me some time to grasp that the real aim was my personal growth as a spiritual director and my confidence in myself as such. I was afraid to expose my own experience of doing direction at first.

John: I felt that reluctance and got impatient with it. She seemed too passive and quiet, and it felt like pulling teeth to find out what she was experiencing. I had to remind myself of our first meeting at times when I got impatient because I would begin to wonder whether I could supervise her.

Rose: I could sense his impatience, and I also felt he was too intrusive and direct. His directness in expressing his feelings both challenged me and made me fearful of him.

In spite of these negative feelings, they continued to grow in their trust of one another—a trust that rested on the working alliance that began to be forged in the faith-sharing experience and the initial meeting. They both felt that the working alliance was finally solidified in a session about the sixth week. (They met weekly for an hour.)

John: Rose was talking about a particular directee who was feeling a lot of pain about her life and her relationship with God. She was talking quietly and unemotionally about her experience with the woman, but I felt that she had some strong feelings of concern for her. She seemed sad and even afraid. When I first asked her how she felt, she quietly said that she hoped the woman would meet God. A few more questions got no further. So I said that she sounded very sad and afraid. She seemed taken aback at first, but then began to express her feelings. Tears came to her eyes.

Rose: What surprised me was John's perception of my feelings. I was somewhat aware of feeling strongly about this directee, but after John said what he felt, it was as though I had permission to admit my feelings to myself and to him. As it turned out, my fears stemmed partly from a lack of trust that God could help this woman out of her sadness.

John: After this session I knew that Rose really had the heart to become a good spiritual director. She felt deeply for this woman and could admit her own fears and lack of faith and ask God's help to believe more deeply.

Rose: Now I was sure that John was on my side and that his directness would be used to help me to become more attuned to my own heart and lived faith.

In the relationship of supervision, resistance to the working alliance will surface as it does in the relationship of spiritual direction, and the resistance will readily take the path of focussing on the person of the supervisor. Transference reactions are also possible here. But the resistance can also focus on the reality aspects of the supervisory situation if the supervisor participates in evaluating whether the supervisee will pass a course or get a degree or certificate of training. Where supervisors have such power, they must work even more carefully to establish the working alliance—an alliance whose basic premise is that the supervisee does not want the degree or certificate if he cannot do the work of spiritual direction. Resistance to supervision, like resistance to spiritual direction, is not only to be expected but indicates that the supervision is proving helpful. The working alliance makes it possible for the supervisor to welcome the resistance and for the supervisee to come to grips with it.

Supervisors who already have a contemplative attitude in their own prayer and work of spiritual direction will find that attitude invaluable for their supervisory work. The same attitude of openness and wonder they find crucial in these other areas of their lives they will find crucial in supervision too. Such an attitude is the opposite of the inquisitorial attitude that supervisees are afraid they will encounter and thus is conducive to an atmosphere of openness and of desire to learn and grow.

The contemplative attitude has no thesis to prove and thus invites sharing. Supervisors with a contemplative attitude listen better as well, pick up vibrations and feelings more easily, and respond to what they hear rather than to their own presuppositions. They raise questions and do not fire accusations. The person who listens contemplatively is more likely to say something like: "I got the feeling that you were nervous as you spoke of the directee's erotic feelings in prayer" rather than: "You sounded defensive when erotic feelings came up" or worse yet: "You're hung up on sex." The person with a contemplative attitude is not a detective or an analyzer, but a listener and a responder, who knows that his responses may be strongly colored by his own expectations and biases and so is appropriately careful about the way he frames them.

One of the dangers of supervision, a danger that is particularly strong when a trusting working alliance has not yet been established, is that supervision will focus almost exclusively on the experience of a person who is absent from the session—the directee. It is safer that way; he or she is not there to get defensive or hurt or angry. Such a focus can be defended on the grounds that supervision is meant to help the directee. But this kind of supervision quickly turns into didactic sessions in which the director reports the experience reported by the directee and the supervisor uses the report to illustrate points of spiritual theory and show the director what he can do or expect next. The reduplicated use of the word *report* in the last sentence indicates the dubious value of the procedure. A report of a report of experience, not experience itself, is under discussion. Furthermore, such a session does not help the director to confront his own angels and demons, his own experience as he directed the person and as he reported the direction experience to the supervisor. He grows in theoretical knowledge and perhaps in practical expertise, but he does not grow in self-knowledge as a spiritual director. The main purpose of supervision, as distinct from courses on the spiritual life, is to help the supervisee to learn how to *be* a more effective director, how to overcome the unfreedoms that keep one from being more effective.[3]

Thus, the focus is on what the director reports about his own experience and on how he reports it. With this focus he will learn something about himself as well as about his directee. The directee's experience will inevitably come into the supervisory hour, and that experience will be examined and questioned in terms of its meaning to the directee himself. But the prime focus will be on how the director listened and responded. A frequently heard question in good supervision is "why?" "Why did I respond in the way I did?," the supervisee might ask himself and the supervisor because the response is troubling him. "Why did you ask questions about her relations with her family?" the supervisor may wonder because he does not understand the pertinence of the questions to the directee's prayer life. But these "why" questions should not lead to fruitless speculation about motives. Rather they should lead to a closer look at the experience of the director in the direction hour as he can recall it. "What went through my mind?" "What was I feeling?" "What happened just before I said that?" Just as questions for discernment in spiritual direction lead a person to look more closely at the experience in prayer and become more fine-tuned in awareness, so too in supervision the questions lead a director to greater awareness of what happens in his direction.

Such questions often lead to the realization that the director acted wisely and for the benefit of the directee's relationship with the Lord. Thus, in the example above, the director might well come to understand even more surely that his intuition about the importance of the directee's family life to her relationship with God was correct. The response to the question might have revealed how crabbed and confining the directee's life was and how much the quality of her prayer life was affected by the quality of her family life. The supervisor's questions, therefore, can result in the supervisee becoming more sure of himself and his intuitions. Good supervision is not only challenging; it is also supportive and strengthening. Directors who are helped to reflect on their work find that such reflection reveals their strengths as well as their weaknesses, their faith as well as their lack of faith.

An extended example may shed light on how supervision works in practice. Again we use the experience of John and Rose—a fictionalized version of an actual supervision process. Here, as elsewhere, we have altered names, age, gender, and circumstances so that the people involved cannot be identified.

We have gradually come to realize the value for supervision of a written report of a particular session of spiritual direction. Immediately after a session of direction the director reflects on what happened and makes some notes of what went on during the session. For supervision he picks out part of one meeting and tries to reconstruct the conversation. He gives the supervisor a copy of this report prior to the supervisory session, and it becomes the main focus of the session unless some other matter is more pressing. Focussing on the reconstructed conversation is one of the best ways of getting at the actual process of direction used by the director. Rose agreed to do such a report for each supervisory session.

In the beginning, the most obvious aspect revealed in Rose's reports was her anxiety to say and do the right thing. As a result of this self-preoccupation, it was difficult for her to really hear the directee and to concentrate on the directee's experiences in prayer or in life generally.

It seems almost universal that when people begin a supervised experience of doing counseling or psychotherapy or spiritual direction they become self-preoccupied. They take on a role and seem to lose for a time the major asset they have for helping other persons—their humanity and their interest in others. In Rose's case, too, it was necessary first of all to help her to trust her own humanity, her own love and concern for the people she was directing.

John recalls that it took hard work to help Rose trust God and her own previous learning and experience as dependable sources of whatever suggestions for prayer she might need to make to a directee. Gradually her need to have answers and solutions diminished. There was less and less need to arrive at a spiritual direction session with a prepared agenda. Rose notes: "John helped me to see the need to pray for trust in God's Spirit, that the Spirit would be present in the interviews to help me and my directees. My own personal spiritual direction focussed on my need and desire to trust God more. As I became more trusting of the Spirit, I found myself more able to enter into another person's experience, no matter how it differed from my own. I got more and more excited about the possibilities of learning about God through listening to the experience of directees."

It seems axiomatic that, generally speaking, the more contemplative one becomes in doing spiritual direction, the more contemplative one becomes in prayer, and vice versa. What also happens, as Rose found, is that in spiritual direction sessions responses, texts, and suggestions for prayer come to mind as they are needed. Directors like Rose have a fund of knowledge and experience that is at their call once they lose their anxiety about what they should say.

Supervision also helps directors to pay attention to their own reactions as they listen to directees. These reactions can be indications of their own faith and unfaith—that is, of those areas where they do believe in the grace and power of God and of other areas where they do not, or at least hesitate to believe. If I am afraid that God cannot heal my anger or even tolerate it, for example, then I will be less able to let another person struggle with his anger in his relationship with God.

Rose came to a realization about herself in somewhat the following way.

She was directing a man who was experiencing a good deal of depression, which was not, however, debilitating. He was actually rather successful in his work and seemed to have a relatively happy family life. One supervisory session went something like this:

Rose: He told me that he tried to use Isaiah 43 for prayer, but just could not get into it. He said he felt like a failure in life and didn't feel that God could have much use for him.

John: Uhuh (with a nod).

Rose: I really felt for him and I reminded him of how a month ago he had been promoted.

John: Why did you say that?

Rose: I felt he was forgetting the good things because of his depression.

John: Did he tell God how he felt?

Rose: I don't know. He didn't mention it.

John: And you didn't ask him? (Nod from Rose) Do you recall how you felt as he was talking?

Rose: (After a few moments of silence) I think I felt sad too and kind of afraid.

John: Afraid?

Rose: Yes, afraid that he'd go into a depression and couldn't get out.

The discussion went on to look at Rose's fear and its relation to her own life and her trust in God. She realized that she did not want to listen to depths of sadness and so tended to try to talk people out of feeling sad. Sometimes, as in this instance, she would not help the person to turn to God and express his sadness and ask for help. Rose was able to look at this tendency in her own prayer and spiritual direction and see it as an instance of practical unbelief. In practice she did not act as though she believed that God could do something about such feelings of unworthiness or uselessness. Prayer and her own spiritual direction helped her to overcome the tendency. As the year progressed, she was more and more able to listen to such experiences and to help people turn to God for comfort and healing. She became more and more a believer in God's desire and ability to comfort the cheerless. Interestingly, as she became freer to listen, more of her directees began to share the dark aspects of themselves with her and with God.

In this example, it is important to note what the focus on Rose's actual experience of direction achieved. It changed her as a director not only in relationship to one directee, but with all her directees. If the focus had been on the directee, she would never have learned certain things about her own existential faith. Because the focus was on her own experience, she did learn things about herself and was able to do something about them in her own prayer and spiritual direction. Let us also underline something else: Rose found that more of her directees began talking about feelings of hopelessness or discouragement once she recognized her limitation and was able to turn to God for help. Often enough, directors unconsciously do not want to hear of certain experiences, and directees react to their attitude, perhaps without even being aware of what is happening. Supervision that focusses on the experience of the director can unearth such blocks and help the director to remove them. The director then finds that he begins to hear more from his directees.

Peer group supervision has been mentioned a number of times. Such groups have been found very helpful in a number of areas. The principles we have enunciated for individual supervision apply equally to group supervision. It is, of course, often more difficult to establish in a group the level of trust that is the basis for a good working alliance. Nonetheless it can be done. We have found that faith-sharing sessions and group dynamics sessions with a facilitator foster the level of trust. One of the clearest indications that trust has been established is the willingness of the group to begin to share their more difficult and troublesome experiences.

The advantage of a group becomes clearest when the level of trust is high. It is then much more difficult to evade the critical issue; someone in the group is almost certain to notice the hesitation or the embarrassment or the odd word that betrays it. Someone is also more likely to notice when the focus has shifted from the director to the directee. An example will illustrate.

Joe, the director, is describing a particular direction session with a married man. The directee's prayer is rather dry, and the Lord seems very distant from him in contrast to his prayer in the past couple of months. At one point the director says to the group: "He mentioned that he had had some marital difficulties, but since he passed over them rather quickly I thought it best not to intrude." After he finishes his presentation, the group begins to wonder what might be the cause of the dryness of the man's prayer. They ask the director questions about the nature of the prayer prior to this week's session and speculate on the possibilities of resistance.

One of the members of the group points out that they are focussing on the directee and then says that she is wondering why the director had not at least said: "Do you want to say anything more about the marital difficulties?" She is also intrigued that the director had said he did not want to "intrude"; the word *intrude* interests her. The director begins to defend himself: "If it had been important, the directee would have said more about it. Besides, I didn't want to seem intrusive." She replies: "Suppose, for example, he had said: 'I got very angry at work last week' and then went on to other matters. Would you be more likely to say to him: 'You said you were angry at work. Do you want to say more about that?' or 'Did that anger come into your prayer at all?' Would questions like those seem intrusive?" Joe pauses and then says: "I can feel some anxiety in me. That example hit home. I don't feel intrusive when anger comes up. I feel queasy about asking about such private things as the relationship between husband

and wife. And sometimes, too, about the relationship between a person and God. I wonder if the dryness has something to do with the marital difficulties."

Since he had not pursued the topic with the directee, he could only speculate. As the group continues its discussion, it becomes clear that a number of them feel intrusive asking questions about close relationships. They conclude that because of their qualms, they may have focussed on the directee's dryness rather than on the director's experience.

In individual supervision the use of the word *intrude* and the slight embarrassment might have gone unnoticed if the supervisor had the same qualms as many in the group. In a group one can count on at least one person noticing that the emperor has no clothes.

Group supervision raises with particular force the question of confidentiality. The question arises, of course, whenever a director seeks supervision. It is easier, however, to understand the use of the individual supervisor. But group supervision can also be understood if proper safeguards are used to cloak identities. Fictionalizing the presentations as we have done in the book is strongly encouraged. Those who participate are bound to the same confidentiality as would be demanded of an individual supervisor. The focus, moreover, is on the director's work, not on the directee, since the process of supervision is aimed at helping directors become more competent. Directees are usually grateful when they know that supervision is occurring if they understand its purpose and the safeguards it employs to ensure their privacy. The director who because of his obligations to confidentiality has some doubt about presenting the case of a particular directee to a group can and should avoid the presentation and seek individual supervision at least until his doubt is cleared up.

One form of group supervision that we have found to be very helpful is the case conference. In the case conference the director presents not a single session but an overview of a case of spiritual direction that covers a number of sessions.

The director reviews the whole extent of a direction relationship to see how it has gone and what factors have led to its present position. The overview gives the director a chance to present his view of the direction so that a number of his colleagues can help him evaluate his work. This help can be particularly useful in clarifying his emotional response to the person he is directing. Another advantage is that everyone present can learn more about the larger processes of spiritual direction—that is, larger than the often rather limited view one gets from the supervision of individual sessions. Moreover, the larger view better enables the participants to relate theories of the spiritual life and the findings of speculative theology to the concrete case. Such case conferences can lead to a more fruitful mutual influence between speculative and practical theology.

12

Conclusion

At the beginning of this book we proposed that spiritual direction could help people find their center in God. Like Thomas More, many modern Christians cannot pin their souls at anyone else's back. They need to find their own center, and spiritual direction is the form of pastoral care whose basic direct purpose is to assist them in that task. The rest of the book has been written to help spiritual directors to fulfill more competently the responsibility that the times and their own calling have placed upon them.

We have hoped to engage readers in a dialogue that can contribute to Christian life and thought. We have tried to describe a spiritual direction that begins with people's experience of God and helps them develop a prayer that springs from that experience. We do not pretend to have written a definitive description of such a spiritual direction. We have rather hoped to invite readers to explore it with us.

But a difficulty often arises when we speak of spiritual direction based on experience. That difficulty can, perhaps, best be illustrated by what often happens when we conduct three-day workshops for people in ministry, the majority of whom are spiritual directors with some experience. Repeatedly the following sequence takes place:

On the first day the participants listen with interest to our exposition of spiritual direction. They sometimes find it strongly attractive. But many of their questions, while pertinent, do not relate to experience. They might ask: "What is the difference between spiritual direction and counseling?" Or: "How do you help a person with a particular problem?"

Participants generally accept with enthusiasm the role-plays we use to exemplify experiences of direction. They may raise questions about the nondirective attitude of the director, but often they identify closely with the person playing the part of the directee.

On the second day the exposition continues to be well received, the questions become more penetrating, and the participants identify more deeply with the directee in role-plays. In small groups, however, when participants themselves take the part of the director, many tend not to focus on the directee's experience or to focus on it briefly and then leave it.

On the third day, usually in the morning, we offer another role-play. This time the reaction is quite different. Participants begin to say: "Up to now I thought I understood, but I realize that I didn't." "At first I couldn't see any difference between the direction I've been used to and the direction you're talking about. I need to go away now and think about it."

This experience, repeated a number of times, has made us wonder. Moreover, in our own discussions of direction we have noticed that we, too, often shift away from experience. As a result of these experiences with ourselves and others, we have come to the conclusion that it is difficult, even for intelligent, practiced ministers, to come to grips with a spiritual direction that is based on religious experience and tries to stay close to it. We have begun to speculate that the deepest reason for the difficulty may well be a persistent reluctance on our part to be open and remain open to the living God.

Whether this speculation is true or not, the experiences just described lead us to ask ourselves what has happened to our readers as they have read this book. Perhaps they have had reactions similar to the workshop participants and may still not be sure that we have described anything in any way different from what they have ordinarily experienced as spiritual direction. Perhaps we have not; but if readers have been attentive in their reading, a dialogue has begun.

It could continue in this way: the reader could go back to the examples, especially the extended examples, and read them again, putting himself or herself in the place of the director, and ask: "How do I react to the direction described here? Is there something here that jars me or that I don't fully understand?" If the reader does notice something unusual, we hope that he will then go back to the exposition and look there for help with his questions. He may agree or disagree with what he finds; in either case the dialogue can continue, especially if further discussion and communication among directors ensues.

Our hope, in other words, is that this book will be definitive for neither its authors nor its readers—that it can represent instead a continuing exploration. Staying close to our experience of life and of God calls on our deepest resources of mind, heart, and ability to relate to others. None of us fully understands his experience or the experience of others. If we can recognize our lack of understanding and let it serve as an incentive to further exploration, we will learn more about experience and be more open to the way God actually draws people. An always increasing understanding and an ever deepening life are the goals.

As the dialogue and exploration continue, both pastoral care and theological reflection can benefit. The divorce of theology from religious experience has begun to be healed, and spiritual directors who are alive to theological issues and regularly in contact with the religious experience of Christians will contribute to further healing.

The dialogue and exploration can also contribute to the elaboration of a more apt language for describing development in prayer and spiritual life. Traditional terminology has often not been the language of relationship. The *Spiritual Exercises* of Ignatius, for example, have usually been described in terms of "weeks." Those who are familiar with the Exercises often speak of a "First Week" or a "Second Week" dynamic. In a language that seems more clearly expressive of the actual experience of retreatants, we would refer to the "First Week" dynamic as that stage when the directee is desirous of, and struggling against, the Lord's willingness to love him or her and save him or her, warts, moles, and all. The great achievement of this dynamic is the directee's freedom to receive love, salvation, forgiveness from the Lord. The "Second Week" dynamic represents the struggle of the retreatant to take on the values of Jesus, identify with him, and care for what he cares for. The achievement is companionship with Jesus, the directee's freedom to give or to serve as Jesus gave and served. Continued attention to experience can help us to develop a new and more expressive developmental language that will benefit both spiritual theology and pastoral care.[1]

To achieve these ends of enriching Christian life and thought, spiritual directors will have to be open to a wide range of people and experiences. Spiritual directors run the risk of gathering around them a small coterie of people, all of the same social class, race, education, milieu, and religious denomination. Indeed, within the same denomination the danger is that the group will all be "professional religious people"—ministers and their spouses, nuns, priests, seminarians, and the like. If this happens, the experiences of a small group of like-minded people run the risk of being considered the only possible experiences of God. Perhaps many ordinary people lose interest in the churches because the experience of the professional class of religious people has become the base upon which pastoral-care approaches and preaching build. How many professional ministers know the religious experiences of the cab driver, the mother of small children, the factory worker, the business person? More and more ordinary people are looking for help with prayer. As they share their experiences of God, the life of the Church will be enriched and spiritual directors will be less likely to make their own experience normative.

Experiences of people in different cultures and countries can open our horizons. Cultural imperialism clashes with a contemplative attitude. The latter is interested in the other's experience, not in fitting that other into one's own mold. A sympathetic and contemplative openness to non-Christian religious experience will also help to broaden horizons.[2] Those who love God want to know more about him.

We need to know how God is experienced by the very poor and destitute. A few directors have begun to work with the destitute. This work is still in its early stages, but where the director's contemplative attitude is well developed, it seems promising.

It is our hope that spiritual direction will become more available to the people of God. If this is to happen, directors will have to learn how to talk about prayer with people who are unused to doing so. They will have to use the language of experience and spend time helping people to believe that their experience is important. Such time will be very well spent. It would have been exciting and informative to listen to the religious experiences of Cesar Chavez, for example.[3]

These last considerations point us towards the relationship between spiritual direction and social justice. The wellspring of Cesar Chavez's campaigns for justice is his spiritual life.[4] The posthumous publication of *Markings* established that Dag Hammarskjöld's work for world peace had been rooted in a contemplative life. There is no doubt that prayer and an active life have often gone hand in hand. Some Christians, however, have feared that the turn to interiority, signalled by the rise of so many contemporary spiritual movements, is leading to a loss of energy needed for the righting of social wrongs. We would like to comment on this question as an appropriate conclusion to this book.

What is the relationship between spiritual direction and social theory and action? A first approximation of an answer comes from a clear view of the purpose of spiritual direction. It is not the spiritual director's task to tell the directee where to put his energies. If the Lord of reality has something in mind, he will communicate it in the directee's relationship with him. The director's task is to facilitate open communication between the directee and the Lord. The large and increasing number of directees who are engaged in one or more areas of the struggle for social justice indicates that they have become aware of the need for social action. In a world crying for justice and for food, and at a time when religious authorities are unanimously urging Christians to join the struggle for justice, it would give pause if a directee's prayer never raised a thought or question about his own part in the struggle. The Christian tradition has rightly been suspicious of a prayer life that showed no concern for others. Spiritual directors, therefore, rightly raise questions about a prayer life that disregards issues of social justice. But they raise them as spiritual directors, not as teachers, preachers, or exhorters.

Secondly, we can say, with Bernard Lonergan,[5] that the person with a converted heart is different from one with an unconverted heart. Both may engage in action for social justice, but their hearts are different. The difference in hearts is what spiritual direction is about. In our experience, active, involved people do not lose their passion for work with and for God's people when they enter into spiritual direction, but they do often lose harshness and contempt for those of different points of view as their hearts are changed.

At the same time, the person who begins spiritual direction today is different from the person who asked Ignatius of Loyola for direction. The consciousness of the need to ground oneself in the interior life is far more widespread in our age. But social theorists also demonstrate how we become so enmeshed with the social, political, and cultural mores and institutions we are part of that the inner and the outer are like the warp and woof of our personalities. And these "public" structures[6] of our experience are as unconsciously operative as any intrapersonal patterns. Indeed, it is more difficult to become aware of these social, cultural, and institutional structures of our experience because they are shared by everyone around us. We have grown so accustomed to certain ways of structuring our experience that we would probably suffer traumatic anxieties if these ways were removed.[7] In other words, the personality patterns which the Lord of reality needs to confront in our age include these public dimensions which also prevent us from seeing him clearly and from seeing his world more clearly. The question social theorists ask spiritual directors is: How do you help people to become aware of these blind spots that hinder them from being more real themselves and letting God be more real to them?

This is a good question. The only answer is that spiritual direction has to remain true to its own inner dynamic, which is to facilitate the relationship between the Lord and the directee and trust that the Lord and life and the other ministries of the Church will also do their work. What is sure is that contemplation does not, in experience, lead people who already have a consciousness of the public dimensions of personality (and of public sinfulness[8]) back to a more interiorized, private kind of piety. Moreover, in experience, as people become more real before God and he before them, radical changes occur; for example, they become more open to the kinds of reading, lectures, and preaching that do challenge their "public" schemata.

Finally, we need to lay to rest a persistent and dangerous idea that borders on a delusion: neither prayer nor spiritual direction gives the answers to all problems. Prayer and spiritual direction are concerned with a relationship, not with magical solutions, and the relationship with the Lord, like any other relationship, is fostered and cherished because of the love of the Other and not because it offers utilitarian advantages such as knowledge of how to vote or how to organize for justice or what social problems to attack first. The person who is in love with the Lord still needs to do his homework if he wants to learn in school or decide which way to vote on a critical issue in local politics. And if organizing slum tenants against unjust landlords is needed, he had better have learned how to go about the job somewhere else than on his knees.

Too often these days religious people justify their decisions by saying they have prayed over them. Hopefully the prayer has helped them have some zest for the choice they have to make, but hopefully, too, they have done their homework well. Prayer—and spiritual direction—will get a bad name if bad judgments and decisions are arrived at and attributed to it. In the last analysis, spiritual direction aims not at producing "right choices," or "good churchgoers," or "active apostles," or "clear-headed decision makers," but at fostering a relationship, a relationship of love. Those who are helped by spiritual direction will, we hope, work for the coming of the Kingdom of God on earth. We know many who do. But the spiritual direction they engage in has left them free to decide.

Notes

CHAPTER 1

1. For example, throughout the excellent articles under the title "Direction Spirituelle" in *Dictionnaire de Spiritualité*, vol. 3 (Paris: Beauchesne, 1957) there is a thread: the aim of spiritual direction is to lead a person to perfection, or to understand the will of God for his or her life and to carry it out. The director must know the person, must instruct the person theologically, must aid the person. The stress is on self-renunciation, practice of virtue, and a life of prayer, but throughout this long article there is very little discussion of a personal relationship with God and of the nature of prayer.
2. See David L. Fleming, "Models of Spiritual Direction," *Review for Religious* 34 (1974): 351–357.
3. The latter phrase appears often in the writings of Karl Rahner.
4. That this feeling is not far from the mark is indicated by the fact that Gustave Bardy (*Dictionnaire de Spiritualité*, op. cit., 1173–1194) takes up the question of whether the directee should take a vow of obedience to the director. He urges great caution but thinks that such a vow may be opportune in some cases.

CHAPTER 2

1. Ernest Becker makes such a point in *Denial of Death* (New York: Free Press, 1973).
2. R. W. Chambers, *Thomas More* (Ann Arbor, Mich.: University of Michigan Press, 1958), pp. 309–310.
3. Paul W. Pruyser, *Between Belief and Unbelief* (New York: Harper & Row, Publishers, 1974), p. 54. Pruyser maintains that until recent times belief was the norm, unbelief a deviant condition in need of explanation.
4. See Josef Sudbrack, *Beten Ist Menschlich: Aus der Erfahrung Unseres Lebens mit Gott Sprechen* (Freiburg im Breisgau: Herder, 1973), pp. 38–44, for a careful and insightful analysis of the modern circumstances of the believer. He develops the ideas presented cursorily in the text.

5. See Paul Ricoeur, *Freud and Philosophy: An Essay on Interpretation* (New Haven and London: Yale University Press, 1970) for a dense and difficult, but penetrating presentation of the problem posed by Freud for the believer today.

6. See Peter L. Berger, *The Sacred Canopy: Elements of a Sociological Theory of Religion* (Garden City, N.Y.: Doubleday & Co., 1967).

7. Peter L. Berger, *A Rumor of Angels: Modern Society and the Rediscovery of the Supernatural* (Garden City, N.Y.: Doubleday Anchor Books, 1970), p. 47.

8. Karl Rahner, *Foundations of Christian Faith: An Introduction to the Idea of Christianity* (New York: The Seabury Press, 1978).

9. Bernard J. F. Lonergan, *Insight: A Study of Human Understanding* (New York: Philosophical Library, 1956).

10. See Thomas S. Kuhn, *The Structure of Scientific Revolutions* (Chicago: The University of Chicago Press, 1962), for a discussion of the notions of paradigm and paradigm shift. For one application to theology see Joseph A. Komonchak, "*Humanae Vitae* and its Reception: Ecclesiological Reflections," *Theological Studies*, 39 (1978): 221–257.

11. Bernard J. F. Lonergan, *Method in Theology* (New York: Herder and Herder, 1972).

12. Joseph Sudbrack dates the dissolution of the unity between dogmatics and spirituality to the twelfth and thirteenth centuries in his article "Spirituality" in *Sacramentum Mundi: An Encyclopedia of Theology*, eds. Karl Rahner et al. (New York: Herder and Herder, 1970), 6: 148–157.

13. St. Athanasius, *The Life of Saint Antony*, trans. and annot. Robert T. Meyer (Westminister, Md.: Newman Press, 1950), pp. 19–20.

14. See for example Marie-Denise Valentin, O.P., in the introduction to Hilaire D'Arles, *Vie de Saint Honorat*, Sources Chrétiennes, no. 235 (Paris: Les Editions Du Cerf, 1977), 39, and Pierre Maraval in his notes to Grégoire De Nysse, *Vie De Sainte Macrine* (Paris: Les Editions Du Cerf, 1971), p. 265, n. 2.

15. Clement of Alexandria, *Christ the Educator*, trans. Simon P. Wood, C.P., in *The Fathers of the Church* 23 (New York: Fathers of the Church, Inc., 1954).

16. See H. I. Marrou, *A History of Education In Antiquity*, trans. by George Lamb (New York: Mentor Books, The New American Library, 1956), pp. 201, 301.

17. Clement of Alexandria, op. cit., pp. 86–89.

18. "The So-Called Letter to Diognetus" in *Early Christian Fathers* 1, trans. and ed. Cyril C. Richardson (Philadelphia: The Westminister Press, 1953), sec. 10, pp. 221–222. For a treatment of the development

of Christian life in the *To Diognetus*, see Irénée Hausherr, S. J., "*La Spiritualité des Premières Générations Chrétiennes*," in A. Ravier, S.J., et al., *La Mystique et les Mystiques* (Paris: Desclée De Brouwer, 1965), pp. 409–460.

19. See Avery Dulles, *Revelation Theology* (New York: Herder and Herder, 1969), pp. 38, 39, 172; Jean Leclerq, O.S.B., *The Love of Learning and the Desire for God: A Study of Monastic Culture*, trans. Catharine Misrahi (New York: Fordham University Press, 1961, 1974), pp. 233–286, 99–100; Louis Cognet, *La Spiritualité Moderne* 3 (Paris: Aubier, 1966), pp. 292–293; "Dogmatic Constitution on Divine Revelation: Vatican II, *Dei Verbum*," in *Vatican Council II: The Conciliar and Post Conciliar Documents*, ed. Austin Flannery, O.P., (Northport, New York: Costello Publ. Co., 1975), ch. 1, no. 6, p. 752 with ch. 2, no. 8, p. 754; ch. 6, no. 21, 23–25, pp. 762–765.

20. Aelred of Rievaulx, "Jesus at the Age of Twelve," in *The Works of Aelred of Rievaulx, 1: Treatises, The Pastoral Prayer* (Spencer, Mass.: Cistercian Publications, 1971), pp. 3–39.

21. Leclerq, op. cit., pp. 106–109.

22. William of St. Thierry, *Exposition of the Song of Songs*, trans. Mother Columba Hart, O.S.B. (Shannon, Ireland: Irish University Press, 1970).

23. William of St. Thierry, op. cit., pp. 46–47 and n. 18, pp. 51–52. See also his *The Golden Epistle*, trans. Theodore Berkeley, O.C.S.O.. (Kalamazoo, Mich.: Cistercian Publications, Inc., 1976), pp. 68–69, 97–98.

24. See Dom François Vandenbroucke, in Dom Jean Leclercq, et al., *The Spirituality of the Middle Ages*, vol. 2 of Louis Bouyer et al., *A History of Christian Spirituality* (New York: The Seabury Press, 1968), pp. 407–409, 481–543.

25. Especially Luis Goncalves da Câmara, *The Autobiography of St. Ignatius Loyola*, trans. Joseph F. O'Callaghan, ed. John C. Olin (New York: Harper Torchbooks, 1974); Ignatius of Loyola, *The Spiritual Journal of St. Ignatius of Loyola*, trans. William J. Young (Rome: Centrum Ignatium Spiritualitatis, 1979); Ignatius of Loyola, *The Spiritual Exercises of St. Ignatius*, trans. Louis J. Puhl, S.J. (Chicago: Loyola University Press, 1951).

26. Luis Goncalves da Câmara, op. cit., pp. 62–71.

CHAPTER 3

1. *Experience* can refer not only to individual experiences, but also to a series of experiences. We speak of a seventy-year-old woman's experience of life. We can also speak in the same cumulative sense of her experience of God.

CHAPTER 4

1. William J. Connolly, "Appealing to Strength in Spiritual Direction," *Review for Religious* 32 (1973): 1060–1063.
2. Psalm 139:1.
3. William A. Barry, "On Asking God to Reveal Himself in the Spiritual Exercises," *Review for Religious* 37 (1978): 171–176.
4. Antoine de Saint-Exupéry, *Le Petit Prince* (New York: Harcourt, Brace, and World, 1943).
5. The fourth-century monks of the Middle Eastern deserts seem also to have had an eye for the beauty of nature. See Derwas J. Chitty, *The Desert a City: An Introduction to the Study of Egyptian and Palestinian Monasticism under the Christian Empire* (London & Oxford: Mowbrays, 1977), p. xvi.
6. This experience of contemplation of Jesus in and through contemplation of the gospels brings one face to face not with a docetist Christ, but with the mystery of a human being to whom one yet says "My Lord and my God." Sudbrack, following Karl Rahner, points out that spirituality has often made the starkness of such a faith harmless by stressing the divinity of Christ; see *Beten Ist Menschlich*, op. cit., pp. 245ff.
7. Ignatius of Loyola, *The Spiritual Exercises of St. Ignatius*, trans. Louis J. Puhl, S.J. (Chicago: Loyola University Press, 1951), no. 49, p. 26.
8. Josef Sudbrack, *Beten Ist Menschlich: Aus der Erfahrung Unseres Lebens mit Gott Sprechen* (Freiberg im Breisgau: Herder, 1973), p. 129.
9. Morton T. Kelsey, *God, Dreams and Revelation* (Minneapolis, Minn.: Augsburg Publishing House, 1975).
10. Contemplation of the Lord can be said to begin with the first interior recognition of God as personal reality, though the directee may for some time not pay much attention to what he may be for him or be saying to him. Clear development of this attitude would not, then, mark the appearance of a new entity, but a new stage of growth.

CHAPTER 6

1. Thomas Merton, *The Seven Storey Mountain* (New York: Harcourt, Brace, 1948), p. 211. Reprinted by permission of Harcourt, Brace, Jovanovich, Inc.
2. Jacques Guillet et al., "Discernment des Esprits," *Dictionnaire de Spiritualité* (Paris: Beauchesne, 1957) 3: cols. 1222–1291; translation of the article by Sr. Innocentia Richards, *Discernment of Spirits* (Collegeville, Minn.: Liturgical Press, 1970).
3. Ignatius of Loyola, *The Spiritual Exercises of St. Ignatius*, trans. Louis J. Puhl, S.J. (Chicago: Loyola University Press, 1951), no. 313–336, pp. 141–150.

4. Thomas S. Kuhn, *The Structure of Scientific Revolutions* (Chicago: The University of Chicago Press, 1962), p.115.

5. Ibid., p. 64. "In science, as in the playing card experiment, novelty emerges only with difficulty, manifested by resistance, against a background provided by expectation."

6. Erving Goffman, *Frame Analysis: An Essay on the Organization of Experience* (Cambridge, Mass.: Harvard University Press, 1974), p. 30.

7. "By a *schema* (plural *schemata*) we mean a structure for organizing experience. A schema gives meaning to events." Harold L. Raush, William A. Barry, Richard K. Hertel, and Mary Ann Swain, *Communication, Conflict and Marriage* (San Francisco: Jossey-Bass, 1974), p. 42. Chapter 3 ("Interpersonal Communication") and Chapter 5 ("Schemata") of this book develop in more detail, and give references to, communication theory and object relations theory. Our presentation is based on the studies which produced that book.

8. "Although anxiety may undeniably at times be a relatively, even severely, disabling symptom, it is nevertheless to be regarded as an affect which is absolutely inseparable from successful growth and maturation in almost every phase of the life cycle. In summary, not all anxiety is to be regarded as pathological." Elizabeth R. Zetzel and William W. Meissner, *Basic Concepts of Psychoanalytic Psychiatry* (New York: Basic Books, 1973), p. 201. A parallel point of view is developed by Kuhn, op. cit., with regard to paradigm shifts (revolutions) in the history of science; crisis has to occur before a new paradigm will even be considered. The classic case is the proposal of a heliocentric astronomy by the Greek Aristarchus in the third century B.C. At the time, the geocentric theory of Ptolemy was not in any crisis and seemed vastly more reasonable. Only eighteen centuries later was there sufficient crisis among astronomers to make them open to the heliocentric theory as proposed by Copernicus.

9. Some of the evidence for these statements is summarized in Raush, Barry et al., op. cit.

10. Spiritual directors will have much to offer to such a developmental religious psychology on the basis of the experiences their directees have with God. We have already made some contributions along this line: W. A. Barry, "The Experience of the First and Second Weeks of the Spiritual Exercises," *Review for Religious* 32 (1973): 102–109 and W. J. Connolly, "Experiences of Darkness in Directed Retreats," *Review for Religious* 33 (1974): 609–615. From a psychoanalytic perspective, Ana-Maria Rizzuto looks at the early development of the God-image in *Birth of the Living God: A Psychoanalytic Study* (Chicago: University of Chicago Press, 1979).

11. J. S. MacKenzie, *Nervous Disorders and Character* (1946), pp. 36–37. Quoted in Henry Guntrip, *Psychology and Religion* (New York: Harper & Row, Publishers, 1957), p. 200. Italics in the original.
12. Luke 10:32–42 (The Revised Standard Version has been used throughout this book.)
13. Mark 10:17–22.
14. Mark 8:31; 9:31; 10:33–34.
15. Mark 8:22–26.
16. Mark 10:46–52.
17. Ignatius of Loyola, *Spiritual Exercises*, op. cit., no. 329, p. 147.
18. In Chapter 10 we shall discuss this topic more fully.
19. Rom. 5:20.
20. See Chapter 9 for a discussion of this concept.
21. William J. Connolly develops this point with regard to facing experiences of darkness in his essay "Experiences of Darkness in Directed Retreats," op. cit.
22. Ignatius of Loyola, *Spiritual Exercises*, op. cit., no. 326, pp. 145–146.

CHAPTER 7

1. See *The Wisdom of the Desert Fathers: Apophthegmata Patrum from the Anonymous Series*, trans. and intro. Sister Benedicta Ward, S.L.G., (Fairacres, Oxford: SLG Press, Convent of the Incarnation, 1975), p. 32, no. 101.
2. Luis Concalves Da Câmara, *The Autobiography of St. Ignatius of Loyola*, trans. Joseph F. O'Callaghan, ed. John C. Olin (New York: Harper Torchbooks, 1974), pp. 23–24.
3. Ibid., p. 33.
4. Ibid., p. 40.
5. Ignatius of Loyola, *The Spiritual Exercises of St. Ignatius*, trans. Louis J. Puhl, S. J. (Chicago: Loyola University Press, 1951), no. 6, p. 3.
6. Gal. 5:22–23.
7. Cf. Ladislaus Orsy, "Toward a Theological Evaluation of Communal Discernment," *Studies in the Spirituality of Jesuits* 5, no. 5 (1973): pp. 173–175.
8. Josef Sudbrack, *Beten Ist Menschlich: Aus der Erfahrung Unseres Lebens mit Gott Sprechen* (Freiberg im Breisgau: Herder, 1973), p. 220.
9. David M. Stanley, "Contemplation of the Gospels, Ignatius of Loyola, and the Contemporary Christian," *Theological Studies 19 (1968)*: 417–443.
10. Thomas Merton, *The Seven Storey Mountain* (New York: Harcourt, Brace, 1948), p. 370. Reprinted by permission of Harcourt, Brace, Jovanovich, Inc.

11. Sulpicius Severus, *Life of Saint Martin, Bishop and Confessor,* trans. Bernard M. Peebles, in *The Fathers of the Church* 7, (New York: Fathers of the Church, Inc., 1949), p. 136.
12. This growth in discernment is one of the most fundamental themes running through the *Autobiography of St. Ignatius of Loyola,* op. cit.
13. Cf. Karl Rahner, *The Dynamic Element in the Church* (New York: Herder and Herder, 1964).
14. Matt. 7:20.

CHAPTER 8

1. Eugene C. Kennedy and Vincent J. Heckler, *The Catholic Priest in the United States: Psychological Investigations* (Washington, D.C.: United States Catholic Conference, 1972), pp. 9–11. Kennedy and Heckler make it clear that as a group priests are ordinary men, i.e., that the proportion of men in the population at large who would be labelled underdeveloped is probably at least as high as it is in this sample of priests.
2. 1 John 4:10.
3. Eph. 2:1–10.
4. John 1:5.
5. Rom. 5:20.
6. Trygve Braatøy, *Fundamentals of Psychoanalytic Technique* (New York: John Wiley & Sons, 1954), p. 2.
7. Jacques E. Levy, *Cesar Chavez: Autobiography of La Causa* (New York: W.W. Norton & Co., 1975), p. 197.
8. For this analysis of the components of warmth we are relying on Edward S. Bordin, *Psychological Counseling,* 2nd ed. (New York: Appleton-Century-Crofts, 1968), pp. 183–212.
9. Ibid., p. 204.
10. Braatøy, op. cit., pp. 50–51. (Italics in the original.)
11. Friederich Wulf, "Die Leitung des geistlichen Lebens und die Sorge um seine richtigen kirchlichen Strukturen," in F. X. Arnold, F. Klostermann, K. Rahner, and I. M. Weber eds., *Handbuch der Pastoraltheologie: Praktische Theologie der Kirche in ihrer Gegenwart,* Band 3 (Freiburg: Herder, 1968), p. 558. (Translation ours.)

CHAPTER 9

1. The concept "working alliance" was coined by the psychoanalyst Ralph R. Greenson. "The working alliance is the relatively nonneurotic, rational relationship between patient and analyst which makes it possible for the patient to work purposefully in the analytic situation." *The Technique and Practice of Psychoanalysis* (New York: International

Universities Press, 1967), 1: 46. Elizabeth Zetzel uses the term "therapeutic alliance"; see Elizabeth R. Zetzel and William W. Meissner, *Basic Concepts of Psychoanalytic Psychiatry* (New York: Basic Books, 1973), pp. 284–301. Though both terms refer to the same thing, we prefer the term "working alliance" for spiritual direction since it avoids the connotations of therapy and a medical model.

2. Ibid., pp. 192–193.
3. Carl R. Rogers, "Therapy, Personality, and Interpersonal Relationships." In Sigmund Koch (ed.), *Psychology: A Study of a Science* (New York: McGraw-Hill, 1959), 3: 184–256.
4. Otto Rank, *Will Therapy and Truth and Reality* (New York: Alfred A. Knopf, 1968). (First English edition 1936.)
5. Peter L. Berger, *A Rumor of Angels: Modern Society and the Rediscovery of the Supernatural* (Garden City, N.Y.; Doubleday Anchor Books, 1970).
6. Rom. 8:15.
7. Rom. 8:26.
8. The term was apparently coined by Karl Menninger. For a very useful discussion of the initiation of the counseling relationship, see Edward S. Bordin, *Psychological Counseling*, 2nd ed. (New York: Appleton-Century-Crofts, 1968), pp. 215–231.
9. Generally speaking, it is advisable for the directee to come to the director's place rather than vice versa. For one thing, the freedom of the directee to come or not come is clearer. Also, the working alliance is clearer to both director and directee if the directee is the one who puts himself out to make the appointment. Transference issues are more easily handled as well. These concepts will be explained in later chapters.
10. The reference is to J. R. R. Tolkien's *The Fellowship of the Ring* (New York: Ballantine Books, 1965), p. 242. The passage is speaking of the ponies who were lost in Bree on the trip to the elf kingdom Rivendell. They were found by Bob and Tolkien opines: "They had to work harder in Bree, but Bob treated them well; so on the whole they were lucky: they missed a dark and dangerous journey. But they never came to Rivendell."
11. T. S. Eliot, *The Cocktail Party*, act I, scene 1, in *The Complete Poems and Plays* (New York: Harcourt, Brace, 1952), p. 306. Reprinted by permission of Harcourt, Brace, Jovanovich, Inc.

CHAPTER 10

1. See Henri Ellenberger, *The Discovery of the Unconscious: The History and Evolution of Dynamic Psychiatry* (New York: Basic Books, 1970).
2. See Elizabeth R. Zetzel and William W. Meissner, *Basic Concepts of*

Psychoanalytic Psychiatry (New York: Basic Books, 1973), for an excellent presentation of psychoanalytic theory, although it does require some prior knowledge of Freudian terminology.

3. See Edward S. Bordin, "The Ambiguity Dimension of Therapeutic Relationships," ch. 6 of *Psychological Counseling*, 2nd ed. (New York: Appleton-Century-Crofts, 1968), pp. 140–165.

4. In his insightful and powerful book *The Denial of Death* (New York: Free Press, 1973), Ernest Becker sees transference as a way of assuaging our fears of death. He tellingly notes the dangers of transferring such needs onto any other human or institution. God as the transference object is healthier, according to Becker.

5. See William J. Connolly "Experience of Darkness in Directed Retreats," *Review for Religious* 33 (1974): 609–615 for a fuller discussion of this mode of directing another.

6. See Ralph R. Greenson, *The Technique and Practice of Psychoanalysis* (New York: International Universities Press, 1967), 1: 348ff for a working definition and illuminating discussion. Lucia Tower also has a fine treatment of countertransference in "Countertransference," *Journal of the American Psychoanalytic Association* 4 (1956): 224–255.

7. To be certain that the reaction is an instance of countertransference, we would need to know more about the director. Countertransference, like transference, is present only when the feelings transferred derive from early relationships in life.

CHAPTER 11

1. One instance of the reality seems to be in the practice of the early Society of Jesus. In his Constitutions, Ignatius of Loyola says of those Jesuits in studies: "After they have had experience of the Spiritual Exercises in their ownselves, they should acquire experience in giving them to others." Then in an expansion note to this paragraph he says: "They could begin by giving the Exercises to some in whose cases less is risked, and by conferring about their method of procedure with someone more experienced, noting well what he finds more useful and what less so." *Constitutions of the Society of Jesus*, trans. George E. Ganss (St. Louis: The Institute of Jesuit Sources, 1970), pp. 202–203, nos. 408–409.

2. For a useful, insightful, and full treatment of supervision in counseling and psychotherapy, see William J. Mueller and Bill L. Kell, *Coping with Conflict: Supervising Counselors and Psychotherapists* (New York: Appleton-Century-Crofts, 1972).

3. We have found in supervising directors that the aspect of their direction that most needs supervision is the central one—the ability to help

directees speak concretely of their experience of God. The resistance of the director to such concrete descriptions of the experience can be both strong and unnoticed. See William J. Connolly, "Spiritual Direction: An Encounter with God," *Human Development* 1, no. 4 (1980): 43–44.

CHAPTER 12

1. James W. Fowler has elaborated a promising developmental theory of stages of faith in *Stages of Faith: The Psychology of Human Development and the Quest for Meaning* (San Francisco: Harper & Row Publishers, 1981).
2. John T. Carmody has described the religious experience of the Buddha and related that experience to the experiences of Jesus in "A Next Step for Catholic Theology," *Theology Today* 33 (1976): 371–381.
3. Jacques E. Levy, *Cesar Chavez: Autobiography of La Causa* (New York: W. W. Norton & Co., 1975). Another fascinating experience might have been provided by the black sharecropper whom Theodore Rosengarten calls Nate Shaw and whose memories of life in Alabama from the turn of the century to the sixties are given in his own words in Rosengarten's *All God's Dangers: The Life of Nate Shaw* (New York: Alfred A. Knopf, 1974).
4. Levy, op. cit.
5. Bernard J. F. Lonergan, *Method in Theology* (New York: Herder and Herder, 1972), p. 271.
6. Peter J. Henriot speaks of the individual, the interpersonal, and the public dimensions of the person in "The Public Dimension of the Spiritual Life of the Christian: The Problem of 'Simultaneity,'" in William R. Callahan and William A. Barry, eds., *Soundings: A Task Force on Social Consciousness and Ignatian Spirituality* (Washington, D.C.: Center of Concern, 1974), pp. 13–14.
7. William R. Callahan speaks of cultural addictions in "The Impact of Culture on Religious Values and Decision-Making," in Callahan and Barry, eds., *Soundings*, op. cit., pp. 8–12.
8. William A. Barry, "The Spiritual Exercises and Social Action: The Role of the Director," in Callahan and Barry, eds., *Soundings*, op. cit., pp. 22–24.

Select Bibliography

Barry, William A., et al. "Affectivity and Sexuality: Their Relationship to the Spiritual and Apostolic Life of Jesuits. Comments on Three Experiences." *Studies in the Spirituality of Jesuits* (St. Louis: American Assistancy Seminar on Jesuit Spirituality, March–May, 1978), vol. 10, nos. 2 and 3.

Connolly, William J., S.J. "Contemporary Spiritual Direction: Scope and Principles." *Studies in the Spirituality of Jesuits* (St. Louis: American Assistancy Seminar on Jesuit Spirituality, June 1975), vol. 7, no. 3.

Connolly, William J., S.J., and Land, Phil. "Jesuit Spiritualities and the Struggle for Social Justice." *Studies in the Spirituality of Jesuits* (St. Louis: American Assistancy Seminar on Jesuit Spirituality, Sept. 1977), vol. 9, no. 4.

Dyckman, Katherine Marie, and Carroll, L. Patrick. *Inviting the Mystic, Supporting the Prophet: An Introduction to Spiritual Direction*. New York/Ramsey: Paulist Press, 1981.

Edwards, Tilden. *Spiritual Friend: Reclaiming the Gift of Spiritual Direction*. New York: Paulist Press, 1980.

English, John, J., S.J. *Choosing Life*. New York: Paulist Press, 1978.

———. *Spiritual Freedom: From An Experience of the Ignatian Exercises to the Art of Spiritual Direction*. Guelph, Ontario: Loyola House, 1979.

Fleming, David L., S.J., ed. *Notes on the Spiritual Exercises of St. Ignatius of Loyola*. St. Louis: Review for Religious, 1981. (This collection contains a number of articles on spiritual direction.)

Gratton, Carolyn. *Guidelines for Spiritual Direction*. Denville, N.J.: Dimension Books, 1980.

Hart, N. Thomas. *The Art of Christian Listening*. New York: Paulist Press, 1980.

Isabell, Damien, O.F.M. *The Spiritual Director: A Practical Guide*. Chicago: Franciscan Herald Press, 1976.

Laplace, Jean, S.J. *Preparing for Spiritual Direction*. Translated by John C. Guinness. Chicago: Franciscan Herald Press, 1975.

Leech, Kenneth. *Soul Friend: The Practice of Christian Spirituality*. New York: Harper & Row Publishers, 1980.

McNeill, John T. *A History of the Cure of Souls*. New York: Harper & Row Publishers, 1951.

Merton, Thomas. *Spiritual Direction and Meditation*. Collegeville, Minn.: Liturgical Press, 1960.

des Places, Edouard, et al. "Direction Spirituelle." *Dictionnaire de Spiritualité*, vol. 3, cols. 1002–1222. Paris: Beauchesne, 1957.

Sullivan, John, ed. *Spiritual Direction*. Carmelite Studies no. 1. Washington, D.C.: Institute of Carmelite Studies, 1980.

Wall, K. A. "Direction, Spiritual." *New Catholic Encyclopedia*. New York: McGraw-Hill, 1976.

Wulf, Friedrich. "Spiritual Direction." *Sacramentum Mundi*, vol. 6, pp. 165–167. New York: Herder & Herder, 1970.

Of related interest:

Alan Jones
EXPLORING SPIRITUAL DIRECTION:
An Essay on Christian Friendship
Examines the human side of the relationship of director and directee
in the light of Christian faith.   160 pp

Lawrence Cada et al.
SHAPING THE COMING AGE OF RELIGIOUS LIFE
A study of the patterns of transition in American religious
communities.   pbk. 197 pp

Bonnell Spencer
GOD WHO DARES TO BE MAN:
Theology for Prayer and Suffering
Draws upon biblical scholarship and contemporary theology to shape
a coherent account of incarnational faith.   220 pp

Sebastian Moore
THE FIRE AND THE ROSE ARE ONE
Spirituality of the cross for contemporary women and men. 158 pp

James C. Fenhagen
MINISTRY AND SOLITUDE:
The Ministry of Laity and Clergy in Church and Society
Probes the continuing self-examination essential to lay and ordained
Christian ministry.   128 pp